DERWOOD, INC.

JERI MASSI

journey**forth**®

Greenville, South Carolina

Derwood, Inc.

Edited by Carolyn Cooper
Illustrated by Guy Porfirio

©1986 by BJU Press
Greenville, South Carolina 29614
JourneyForth Books is a division of BJU Press

ISBN 978-0-89084-323-9
Printed in the United States of America

35 34 33 32 31 30 29 28 27 26 25

Contents

Dedicated to
Karen Wolff Wilt
and
The "Inkeepers"

PART ONE

ONE
HOW EVERYTHING STARTED

A class trip to a button factory may not be tons of fun, but in my book, it's better than math class any day. And this one class trip had its surprises. For one thing, while the thirty-two of us and Miss Creason were waiting inside the lobby of the big old building, we could hear people arguing. It seemed like somebody had forgotten to announce the seventh-grade class of Peabody Christian School.

Then this lady came out of an office. She was wearing a white coat over her clothes.

"Welcome to Peabody Buttons, Incorporated," she said, like nothing was wrong. She smiled at us. "Boys and girls, I'm your tour guide. Walk this way, and please keep your hands and clothes at a safe distance from the machinery."

All of us girls scrunched our skirts in with our hands, and the class followed her out into the factory. At first it was fun to watch the big automatic presses going up and down and in and out, but I got a little thirsty, so I looked around and spotted a water fountain over in a corner. I decided to get a drink.

I leaned over the old cooler, swung my hair out of the way, and took a long drink. Then above the water fountain I noticed a production chart on the wall, and I tried to figure out how to read it. When I turned around to go back, I didn't see my class.

At first I felt scared, like I had been left behind, but then I decided to cut through some of the alleyways between the machines. I thought I would have a better chance of spotting my group.

I tried that for a while, but I got lost. I had just read a book about some guy stranded in the desert who had eaten crayons and flour paste while waiting to be rescued. So I was wandering around in this big building, telling myself I would have to spend my life eating button paste (if there is such a thing) to stay alive until somebody found me. And then all of a sudden our tour guide came tearing around the corner, furious.

I was about to tell her how glad I was to see her, when she picked me up by my coat lapels so that my toes were off the floor, and she pinned me against the wall. I'm not a really big girl, but still, she must have been strong. Her elbows knocked the breath out of me.

"What are you doing snooping around here?" she asked. "How did you get away from the others?"

I was scared, especially with her angry breath in my face and her arms pinning me into the wall. "I got a drink," I gasped.

Her eyes stared down into mine, and she looked so cruel and angry that my fear came up in my throat, and I yelled for help. Just as quickly she dropped me back onto the floor, and my teacher, Miss Creason, came around the corner. Miss Creason was stout and strong, and she coached girls' athletics. I was glad to see her.

"Here's your lost girl," the tour guide said, her fierceness turning to sternness. "I caught her trying to play with one of the machines and pulled her back just in time."

"Penny!" Miss Creason started to scold me.

I could have spoken up right then, but I was so scared I didn't say a thing. I just let my teacher reprimand me. But then when she saw how frightened I was, she must have thought she'd been too harsh. She just sort of fussed a little more, patted my hand, and brought me back to the group. But all through the rest of the miserable tour, I felt that tour guide's eyes on me. I was never so glad to get out of a place as I was to get out of that factory. And I was still so scared that I just tried to push everything out of my mind. I didn't tell anybody—not even my brother Jack, and I usually end up telling Jack just about everything. I didn't want to think about that woman and how cruel she looked.

It wasn't until months later that I found out who she was.

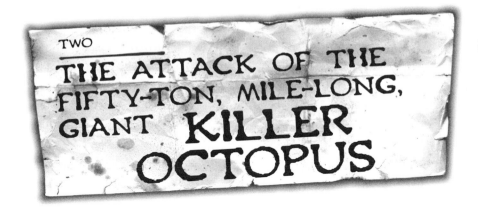

TWO
THE ATTACK OF THE FIFTY-TON, MILE-LONG, GIANT KILLER OCTOPUS

That winter my dad took us up to spend weekends at a cottage on Big Sand Lake. One of his clients had rented it to him.

The six of us spent the first morning huddled at the front window, looking out at the wasteland of snow and ice and wishing we were back in Peabody.

"If we go out there," my brother Jack whispered, "Our toes will freeze and turn black and drop off one by one."

"They will *not*," I whispered fiercely.

"They will too. It happened to this guy I read about. He crashed his plane in the snow, and then his toes dropped off one by one."

"Is that make-believe?" my littlest sister wanted to know.

"Yes," I quickly reassured her.

"It is not!" Jack exclaimed.

"It is too, even if you don't think it is. You got the story wrong."

"Are there polar bears up here?" Freddy asked. Freddy was five.

"Let's watch and see," I suggested. "And let's all be quiet."

My mom and dad had this thing about fresh air. They were always pushing us out into it. At the moment the air was a little too fresh for me, so I hoped if we were quiet they wouldn't notice us.

For a while we watched the barren snow and imagined polar bears sneaking around the cottage, lurking behind drifts, watching and waiting. Then suddenly the quiet was disturbed by a scratching sound on the door. Freddy squealed.

I said, "Shhhhh!" really loud, and Mom came to the front room and opened the door. She let in Sherwood Derwood, our polar cat. Sherwood meowed and started picking bits of ice from her paws with her tongue and teeth.

"Why aren't you outdoors in the fresh air?" Mom asked. "I was just going out myself."

Caught again. We struggled into our coats and scarves and went out on the porch. We huddled around the window, this time looking in. Dad came out, bundled up in his coat and hat.

"Nobody, but *nobody* is up here," he said grandly with a sweep of his arm. "Now for once the Derwood clan has some place big enough to hold them all! I want you kids to work together on Derwood, Incorporated."

Derwood, Incorporated was Dad's idea. Since almost everybody in my family is a half brother or half sister to everybody else, he wanted us to feel close. That was why he was always calling us Derwood, Incorporated.

It takes some figuring to work out just who is who in the family. My father and mother were married in New York. I was born first, and my brother Jack

came a year later. But when I was five years old, my mother died in a car accident, and then my father moved to Wisconsin.

That was where he later remarried a widow with a four-year-old girl, Jean. Jean became my first sister. Dad adopted her so that she could have our same name.

Then my father and my second mother had three more children: Freddy and Renee—the twins—and Marie. That makes six, and that's Derwood, Incorporated.

"You have the whole beach and the woods for hiking and exploring," Dad told us.

"How nice," Jack said politely. "And it's only twenty degrees out here!"

Dad caught the sarcasm, but he was feeling too expansive to comment on it. "Yup, only twenty degrees. Perfect weather, once you've been warmed up by a little exercise. Let me show you, Jack." He handed him a snow shovel. "Go dig out the car. And just remember, I can always find *something* to keep you warm if it gets too cold for you."

Defeated, Jack shuffled over to the car. Although we had arrived only the night before, the poor car was almost buried.

"Any other comments?" Dad asked cheerfully.

"Oh, noooo, Dad!" the five of us chimed in.

"Good. I'll give you five minutes to start enjoying the great outdoors—or else."

"Or else what, Daddy?" Freddy asked innocently. Freddy was too young to understand hints of possible judgments to come.

"Or else you'll all be shoveling out the state of Wisconsin!" Dad said, picking him up and swinging him. "Now, everybody into the snowdrifts! I'll play with you as soon as I shovel a walk for your mother."

We tumbled down off the porch in a hurry. Pretty soon the five of us were building a snow fort while Jack shoveled out the car.

Dad finished the walk about a half hour later. "How do you like the weather now, son?" he called.

"Why, it's glorious, Dad, just glorious!" Jack called back. "I feel like a new man already!"

"I knew you'd like it after you thought about it a while." Dad brought the shovel he'd been using on the walk and gave Jack a hand with the car. That meant the punishment was over—now it was just work.

The first weekend was a success, but it became clearly understood that we were all going to hate the cabin unless we worked together on liking it. Mom and Dad had snowball fights with us, and we even checked out library books on snow sculpture. After three weekends of struggle and failure, we managed to build a halfway-believable snow gorilla. Just before we left that Sunday morning, we all posed around it while Dad took a time-exposure picture. Jack even put Sherwood on the gorilla's shoulder. We knew that the sun and wind would probably destroy our work of art before Derwood, Incorporated returned to Sand Lake next Friday.

* * * * * * *

It was on a dreary, barren weekend that Jack invented the fifty-ton, mile-long, giant killer octopus stories. He and I built a bonfire on the beach late that Saturday afternoon just as the sky was clearing and night was falling. When we were all huddled close, he began his story.

"Once upon a time, last month, a mad scientist up the street from us—"

"Is this make-believe, Jack?" Freddy whimpered.

"Yes, it's make-believe, Freddy. Come sit on my lap," I said.

"Anyway, up the street—"

"The street here, or the street back in Peabody?" Jean asked.

"Back in Peabody, of course," Jack told her. "The big white house on the corner, the one with the windows blocked up with cardboard. Anyway, a mad scientist lived there. He had no hair on top of his head, but all around the sides, it stuck out like bristles. His eyes bulged out like this—" Jack pulled the lids under his eyes down. "And his teeth stuck out like this—" His upper lip curled up. "And he watches out a little hole in the cardboard over the windows—" Jack rolled his eyes back and forth. "He's lookin' for little boys and girls—"

Freddy squealed at Jack and hugged me.

"This guy's supposed to be a mad scientist, not an ogre," I snapped. Creepy stories still made me think back to that factory and the angry tour guide.

"Right," Jack agreed. He went on. "So one day, this traveling salesman knocks on the door—BAM! BAM! It echoed and echoed, like the hallways in that big old house went on forever. BAM! BAM! Bam! Bam! bam! bam!

"And the mad scientist comes walking down the dark steps—creeeeeeak! creeeeak! creeeeeeak! And he says, 'Who's there?' And the traveling salesman says, 'Joe Schmoe, the traveling salesman.'

"And the scientist says, 'What are you selling?'

"And the salesman says, 'Tropical fish!'

"So the scientist lets him in—creeeeeeak!—and then closes the door behind him, and ever . . . so softly . . . he locks it . . . *click!* Then he says to the salesman, 'Pardon me, but what's your hat size?'

"'That's awful personal, why do you ask?' says the salesman.

"'Oh, I was just wondering. I've been doing some brain research upstairs in my laboratory. You have an interesting head, that's all. I suppose there's a brain inside—a nice brain, I mean.'

"'I suppose there is,' says the salesman. 'Could I interest you in some fish? I have some right here in a tank in my briefcase.'"

Jack added a few sticks to the beach fire. The afternoon light was failing, and the sky was nearly clear now. I wanted to suggest singing or a game or something,

but I knew the little kids wouldn't let Jack stop before the story was ended. Soon he continued.

"So the scientist says to the salesman, 'Please sit down,' and they go into the living room. Cobwebs are hanging down, and old wallpaper is peeling off in long strips. The room is dark, too.

"'What sort of fish would you like to see?' asks the salesman in a shaky voice, as he notices the eerie room.

"'Well, I'm much more interested in your head, Mr. Schmoe,' the scientist tells him.

"'Oh dear, I couldn't sell you my head,' the salesman says. 'You see, I don't get a commission on that. But I do have a very nice blowfish here—from off the coast of Africa—'

"But now he's scared. He's thinking of how the scientist locked that door. And then the scientist starts taking operating stuff out of his pocket. 'Why, it wouldn't hurt a bit,' the scientist says.

"'You really don't want to buy a blowfish, do you?' the salesman asks. And he laughs real nervously.

"'Why no, I don't. I've caught something bigger than a fish,' the scientist says, and stands up, laughing. He walks towards Joe—creeeeak, creeeeak, creeeeak! But Joe's got a good head on his shoulders—which he plans on keeping. He pulls a baby octopus out of his briefcase and flings it right at the scientist—splat! The octopus lands on his shoulder and wraps its legs around his neck, four on each side." Jack suddenly let out a shriek. Everybody huddled closer to me.

"That's how the scientist screamed. Joe runs to the door, but he can't unlock it. So he runs up the stairs to the scientist's laboratory, and he slings his briefcase through one of the covered windows—SMASH! And he sees trees right by the window, so he squiggles through, climbs down a tree, and gets away. And he has his company bill the scientist for all the fish he lost when he threw his briefcase out the window. The End."

"What happened to the scientist?" Jean asked.

"He finally pulled the baby octopus off and washed it down the sink. Ah! But little did he know—the octopus drank up all the radioactive chemicals the scientist had dumped down the drain. It got washed into the pipes, and its big round head began to pulse and throb—brum brum—brum brum—boom boom—Boom Boom—BOOM BOOM! And it grew and grew down in the pipes—"

By this time Renee was in my lap, too. Marie had her arms around me, and I had one around her, and even Jean was huddled up against me. They felt pretty secure all scrunched up on me, but I could hardly breathe. And my legs were falling asleep. It was nearly dark by now.

"And it kept growing and growing," Jack went on, "and swimming around the water system of Peabody, Wisconsin, and nobody really knows much about it. But every now and then . . . when somebody's leaning over a sink brushing his teeth . . . a long, thin octopus arm slides up the drain—"

Freddy started crying.

"No it doesn't. No it doesn't, Freddy," Jack said. "It really doesn't."

"It's just a story, Freddy," I told him. "Jack told you at the beginning that it was a once-upon-a-time story." But Freddy was crying in earnest, and the beach had become dark and eerie, so we put out the fire and trudged back to the cottage.

"This is wonderful!" I muttered. "I know where everybody will sleep *tonight!*" And I glared at Jack.

"See how pretty the stars are, Freddy?" Jack said.

Freddy sniffed. "Is Orion's Belt out tonight?"

"Yes." Jack swung him out of my arms, and I picked up Marie. Jack showed us the constellations to calm everybody down.

By the time we got home for supper, Jack had managed to get the little ones calmed down, but they were tired out and clinging to either Jack or me like cement.

"That's what I like to see," Dad said, beaming at Jack and me as we entered. "Everybody having a nice time together."

By dinner time everybody was cheerful, and later I helped Mom put the three younger ones to bed. Nobody said anything about the fifty-ton, mile-long, giant killer octopus, but sure enough, not long after I had gone to bed, Jean came in. "Hi, Penny. Are you lonely?"

"No," I told her.

She looked down.

"Oh."

"But I guess you are." I knew what she was up to.

Hopeful, she looked up.

"Yeah."

"Well—come *on*. We may as well get this over with."

She climbed into the other side of the bed.

A minute later, Marie came in. Being the youngest, she took the direct approach by crying as soon as she walked through the door and climbing into my arms. "I'm scared!"

"Okay, okay, you can sleep in here." After all, she was only four and not really big enough to handle a killer octopus.

Freddy and Renee, the twins, came tearing in as soon as they heard Marie being allowed in. "We had a bad dream; we had a bad dream!" they wailed.

"Well, get in."

I finally got everybody settled, tucked in, kissed, and comfortable (everybody except me). "I'm glad it's a queen-sized bed," I mumbled. "We've got almost everybody in the whole castle." Just as I lay back down with Marie's elbows in my side and Renee's cold heels in my shins, I heard a long, low, almost musical sound coming from Jack's room. He was snoring peacefully.

This started the reign of the fifty-ton, mile-long, giant killer octopus. Every Saturday afternoon my brother and sisters begged Jack for another story, and every Saturday night at the cottage, guess who had two-thirds of the family sleeping with her?

Jack finally did me a favor by telling the kids that the giant octopus loved sugar more than anything else. People who understood that little-known fact could get rid of the octopus by giving it a few tablespoons of sugar. Soon even Marie felt pretty safe as long as she knew there was sugar in the house to give the octopus in case it should turn out to be real.

Meanwhile, Jack moved his octopus headquarters from Sand Lake to the house in Peabody. It was Jack's job to fill up the bathtub for Freddy's bath. One week night he tied a cold sponge to the drain in the bathtub. Freddy stepped in that night, and Jack screamed, "Oh no! The giant killer octopus! It's coming up the drain!" just as Freddy's bare foot touched the sponge.

Freddy almost didn't live to be six. He let out a yell and tore down the stairs into the kitchen.

"I—I was just—just kidding!" Jack was gasping with laughter as he followed. "Come back, Freddy. It was a sponge!"

I'd run into the kitchen after Freddy, but I was just in time to see him dart out the other door. He had the sugar bowl.

"Freddy, wait!" I yelled. Too late. He ran into the downstairs bathroom, and I heard the toilet flush. I ran in just in time to see Freddy, clad like Tarzan in his towel, holding the now-empty sugar bowl, looking at us with satisfaction. "I sent it half a bowl. Is that enough?"

A person might think that Jack was cured after all of that, but soon he was ready for someone else to make contact with the fifty-ton, mile-long, giant killer octopus. Only now he knew better than to do it to the three younger kids.

The next Monday morning while he was at the kitchen sink running the water, I came in to get some water for Mom's tea. "Why are you filling the sink so full?" I asked.

"Huh?" He snapped on the light above the sink and looked down. By habit my eyes followed his when he glanced down into the sink.

I screamed at the sight of a green tentacle coming up out of the drain. Next thing I knew I'd flung the teakettle into the water. Jack and I both got splashed, but he was bent over laughing and didn't care. "Man, did you jump! I've never seen anyone jump so high in my life!"

I felt like a fool—after all, I *knew* the octopus was make-believe. I lifted out the kettle and looked down to see what had tricked me. Jack had fastened a long, narrow spinach leaf to the drain plug. Floating upright in the water, it looked like the tip of a giant tentacle.

"Jack!" I yelled.

"Oh, Penny, it was so funny! C'mon, can't you take a joke? I only did it because I thought you would laugh, too."

"You did it because you thought I would fall for it."

He was apologetic and charming at the same time. "Let's play the joke on Jean. You get her over by the sink and do what I did to you."

"And what are you going to do?" I asked.

"Hide in the cabinet under the sink and make gurgling noises like an octopus coming up the drain."

"Hmmm, well, okay." I should have known better. Why did I let Jack talk me into things?

Jean would be coming in any minute to set the breakfast table. Jack quickly crawled into the cabinet and shut the doors. I stood over the sink, whistling as I pretended to clean the teakettle. Jean came in and pulled some plates down from one of the cabinets above the kitchen counter. As I watched, I wondered what would happen if she dropped them when she saw the octopus feeler. But then I decided that even Jean couldn't be *that* giddy.

"Penny," she said to me, "why are you washing the teakettle before breakfast?" Her eyes glanced at the sink, and she saw the tentacle. Just then, Jack reached out from the cabinet and grabbed Jean's ankle. He was wearing one of Mom's rubber gloves.

"Yagh!" Jean shrieked. I learned right then never to underestimate Jean's giddiness. The whole stack of plates flew straight up and came straight down. Somehow I caught them before they hit the edge of the sink.

"Daaaaaaad!" Jean yelled. I could hear Jack in the cabinet, laughing his heart out. Ha ha. I just realized I had been stupid twice. Now we were both going to get into trouble over his octopus jokes.

THREE

THE RETURN OF THE GIANT OCTOPUS

That afternoon, as we were shoveling out our cars and the neighbors' cars and their neighbors' cars, I gave Jack a piece of my mind.

"I can't believe it is twelve degrees out here, and I'm stuck shoveling snow with you because I was dumb enough to play a practical joke on my poor little sister Jean."

"You'd better quit jabbing that shovel into the snowdrift so hard, or you'll be digging out the car's seat covers," Jack said through his scarf. "The way I see it, Dad will run out of cars to be shoveled pretty soon." He grunted as he lifted out a big wad of snow. "After this let's go get some hot chocolate. I'll treat."

I wondered what he was up to, but I wanted some hot chocolate, so I agreed to go up to the quick mart with him.

An hour later we finished digging out the last car, put the shovels away, and walked up to the quick mart together. Jack ordered a regular hot chocolate, but since I was so mad at him, I ordered a large one just because he had to pay for it like he'd promised.

"Well, I do keep my promises," he said as he paid for it. "We'll take two soft pretzels, please, mister," he told the cashier. He paid for them, too. I knew he was sorry and was trying to make up for it. Jack never spends money without a reason.

We walked back outside into the cold afternoon and sat down on the frozen curb. "Are you mad at me?" he asked.

"I'm trying not to be. You're a good kid, but you did get me in trouble." I looked down at the rich dark chocolate in my cup. "This sure is good," I told him.

"Yeah, we haven't done this in a long time," he said. "We used to do it all the time when we were shining shoes."

"That's probably why we never made much profit," I suggested.

Jack had gone into business for himself last summer, shining shoes. He had cut me in for a third of the profits just for hanging around to keep him company and get him his lunch. It had passed the time in the summer and fall, and we had gotten to know a lot of people.

We would have done a better business shining shoes in the business district where clean shoes are important, but it was too far to walk, so we had settled on the sidewalk in front of the quick mart. There were other stores around—a mattress place, a launderette, a bank, one small office building, the old train station, and even a few little businesses—all within sight of the quick mart.

"We ought to go back into business," he said. "Think of all those boots."

"Nobody on this street makes much money except for the quick mart and the bank," I told him. "Everybody else is going broke."

Once, this little street had been the only business district in Peabody, but those days were long gone. The housewives kept their savings in the little bank, and everybody used the quick mart to pick up little odds and ends like a quart of milk here, a loaf of bread there, or a newspaper. Kids went in a lot for hot chocolate and soft pretzels. But there was only one passenger train a day, and the office building and other small stores were seldom used. Most people did business at the new shopping mall near the interstate.

The mattress place was a two-story wreck. Huge chips of tan-colored paint were peeling off of it. Its upstairs windows had been stuffed with cardboard and rags where the glass had broken out. Some starving artist had painted a sign of a mattress with eyes and a mouth and two little hands. The mattress was holding a candle in one hand and yawning as though inviting people to come in off the street and go to sleep. That enormous cartoon was the one thing halfway funny or charming about the store. Everything else looked sad and run-down.

Every time I looked at that old wreck of a place, I wondered how they managed to stay in business. I don't think I ever saw anybody buy a mattress from the place. While Jack and I had been shining shoes, we had noticed a delivery truck pulling up to it on Monday mornings to drop off a load of mattresses. We figured the place had to have the biggest surplus of mattresses in the world. Maybe when the shopkeeper got bored, he went into his basement and jumped on mattresses.

"Come on," Jack coaxed me. "We could go into business again. Maybe we could earn enough money to do something."

"Like what?"

"Like—like—like bribing Dad to let us all stay home some weekend. I could play hockey with the guys, and you could have a whole night without the little kids jabbing you in bed. We'll give him ten dollars to stay home from Big Sand Lake."

"We couldn't earn ten dollars shining shoes if we worked until Labor Day—1992."

"Worth a try," he told me. Where money is concerned, Jack is what my teacher calls "an eternal optimist." I'm not sure what it means, but it must be true, because Jack always has a new way to earn money.

"Hey, look!" he exclaimed, pointing past me. "Here comes Sergeant McKenna! Hey, Sergeant!"

Mr. McKenna was a deacon in our church, and he worked for the police department. He used to be just Officer McKenna, but he had been promoted to sergeant. We didn't see him much driving around in his police car anymore. Now he worked at his desk most of the time.

"Hey, Penny! Hey, Jack!" he called to us. He was wearing plain clothes instead of his uniform.

"How's the shoe-shine business?" he asked us.

"Aw, we haven't shined shoes in months," Jack told him. "I'm trying to talk Penny into going back into business with me."

"Sure!" Sergeant McKenna said. "You kids ought to do it. People depended on you."

"Not much," I told him. "We didn't get many customers."

"Maybe you'd do it as a public service," he told us. "I need somebody to keep an eye on that mattress store. Looks like a hide-out if I ever saw one."

Jack looked up, startled.

"Oh, come on," I said to Mr. McKenna.

He shrugged and smiled, then walked into the quick mart. Jack turned to me, begging. "Let's try it, Penny. We can watch the mattress store. This is even better than the killer octopus!"

"I'm not sure he was serious, Jack."

"Sure he was serious. It was a tip-off! Let's do it!"

"Well—okay." I didn't really believe it was a hide-out, but I figured if Jack was shining shoes, he would be too busy to play any more killer octopus jokes. Besides, he'd keep buying me hot chocolate and pretzels while I was with him. Not a bad way to pass the time between school and supper.

We asked Mom and Dad if we could go back into business.

"Don't you think you'd make more money shoveling sidewalks and driveways?" Dad asked.

"Oh, I've done enough snow shoveling," Jack groaned. He was right about that.

"Won't you be too cold?" Mom asked.

"We sit on the beach at Sand Lake for hours telling stories," I said. "We never get too cold up there."

"And making money has a way of warming me up," Jack added.

"Hmm, well, I guess it's all right," Dad said. "I prefer shoe shining to monster making."

"The trick," Jack told me the next day as we set up the box and stool on the sidewalk. "The trick to good shoe shining is to really act the part."

"How?"

"Did you know that decades and decades ago when people emigrated to America, their kids would shine shoes to make a living?"

"Really?" I couldn't understand where Jack got all his information. I didn't remember reading that in my sixth-grade history book.

"Yeah, people came from Lithuania, Poland, Hungary—all sorts of places. The men worked in factories, and the kids shined shoes or sold newspapers to help out. So let's you and me pretend we're Hungarian kids shining shoes. Okay-ski?"

"What?"

"Come on, act like you're from another country. Use an accent-ski. When people come up, say, 'Hey, Meester, shineski shoeski? Only a quarterovitch!'"

"A quarterovitch?"

"Hungarian for a quarter."

"That's not Hungarian for a quarter. Jack, you don't know what a Hungarian accent sounds like. People will think we're crazy."

"No they won't. Here's a quarterovitch. Go get me a pretzel-ski."

"Say please."

"Please-ski."

"Can I have one too?"

He flipped me a quarterovitch. "Sure-ski."

When I came out with the pretzels, Jack was calling out to two men coming up the sidewalk. "Hey, Meesters! Shoeski shineski? Only a quarterovitch!"

I melted back inside until they passed. I pretended to look at candy bars, waiting for them to come inside and buy whatever they had come for.

The door swung open. "Hey, Ron, come out here and listen to this goofy kid!" one of the men called to Ron Scott, the storekeeper.

Mr. Scott grinned at me. "I wonder who that could be?" He went out to watch, and after a minute I followed him.

Jack was cracking the rag by this time, briskly skimming it back and forth over the other man's shoe and then snapping it straight out.

"I'm a shinee shoeskis presto adagio, Meester, ey? El hombre ragio strikes like-a lightning, eh?"

"Kid, you're a scream!" the man laughed.

"Hey, he sounds like a Spanish matador in a Chinese restaurant just outside of Budapest!" Mr. Scott called. I melted back inside.

Jack had those men out there for a half hour while I memorized the ingredients on every candy bar in the store. When they finally left, I went outside with the two cold pretzels.

"Have you no self-respect?" I asked him.

"The guy tipped me a dollar. For that much money I can fight down my self-respect. He says he'll bring some friends over here the next time. We're in business again!" He cracked his rag. "If I could teach Harry a few tricks, we could expand even more." Harry was Jack's hamster and—happily—Harry had already proved to be untrainable. Jack was only keeping him to see if he could break the record for the world's longest-living hamster.

"Have you been watching the mattress place?" Jack asked.

"Of course not. Sergeant McKenna was just joking about that place because it looks so run-down."

"Baloney. It was a tip-off."

"It was a joke!" I argued.

"A tip-off!"

"You've been reading too many detective books," I told him.

"Ha-ski!" he shouted. "I hate detective books! You're the one who always has your nose buried in an Amy Belle book!"

His answer stung me. I loved reading detective stories, especially the Amy Belle series, and Jack was always poking fun at them. "Well, just forget the mattress place," I said.

"I'm going to ask Sergeant McKenna about it when I see him at church. He wasn't joking when he said it," Jack told me.

I didn't want to fight with him, so I stopped arguing. We got a few more customers, and then it was time to go home.

"If only we had some excuse to go inside that place," Jack said wistfully, nodding at the mattress store as we packed up.

"Forget it, Jack!" That mattress place reminded me a little bit of the button factory—dark and run-down. It probably had tour guides lurking behind the windows. We set off walking for home.

"I guess I should forget it," he agreed. "I wouldn't want to be kidnaped and held for ransom or anything like that. What if Dad had to sublease that cottage for the rest of the winter just to pay for me?"

"I'd kidnap you myself if it would get rid of that cottage."

"You're all heart."

"That way the money would stay in the family," I told him.

"Uh-oh," he said, nodding up the road.

"What—oh?"

"Here comes Annette." He stifled a sigh. Annette lives on our street and goes to our church. Most of the time she's okay—shares her jump rope with my little sisters and lends me her books, but sometimes she gets stuck on certain ideas.

She used to keep track of who got the memory verses right in Sunday school and who always muffed them. She'd come up to the teacher, Mrs. Bennett, and say, "Hey, guess what? Penny Derwood got her verses wrong *five* weeks in a row, Teacher. I kept count for you." Then she'd smile real sweetly like she was doing it for your own good. She only did it to me once.

But I felt sorry for the nervous kids or the new ones who always got their verses wrong. Annette would listen real carefully to everybody reciting.

"Uh-oh, I can see Annette's antennae going up," Jack used to whisper when we were all in the same class one summer. "Let's see if I can jam the airwaves." And he would start coughing in the back of the room so that whoever was reciting could do it without fear of Annette.

But Mrs. Bennett usually noticed Jack more than she noticed Annette, and she would ask him to be quiet, and—being Jack—he would.

Finally one day Gaspar Pablo Garcias said his verse for the first time in perfect King James English. That was a first for Gaspar because English was only his second language, but Annette had piped up, "Don't you think he said it too fast, Teacher? I don't think he got the punctuation quite right."

Happily, Gaspar didn't speak English well enough to follow what she'd said. He'd been concentrating too much on the verse to listen to her. So when he saw Mrs. Bennett smiling at him with that wet look in her eyes and heard Annette pipe up, he only beamed at Annette and said, "Gracias, Annette, my mother and father—they also help me say it this week, to get my star in Sunday school."

Mrs. Bennett called him her "dear blessed boy," and it took her several minutes and the rest of a box of tissues before she could go on with the lesson. A person gets used to those things with Mrs. Bennett. You should see her at weddings.

After that particular day Annette would only sniff and say, "Well, of course he *tried* hard. It just didn't seem perfect to me." For a long time she kept her mouth shut when we were saying our verses, and Jack no longer had to "jam the airwaves."

But she also had this thing about adoption. She used to come up to me and say, "I heard my parents talking, and you know what they said? They said you were adopted. They really did. You're adopted. Did you know that?"

Of course the first time she said it my heart went into my throat because my mom isn't my mother by birth. When Annette told me I was adopted, I thought for a minute that maybe my mom had adopted us and hadn't told us yet.

Of course after that first thought I realized that Annette was just saying it. I could see that she didn't know anything about Mom being my second mother. I'm a year older than Annette and usually can see right through her. So I didn't fall for it, but it did annoy me more than it should have, and I don't know why.

When Jack was about eight years old, she'd tried it on him. He had looked surprised and then said, "Adopted? Am I really? Well! Okay." Then he'd said, "What's 'adopted'?"

Annette thought he really didn't understand, but I knew that Jack, even then, was picking up some points of sarcasm. I shouldn't have been happy about that, but I was.

A couple years went by before she tried it on Jean. It really bothered Jean, and so Jack and I got mad when Annette would tell her she was adopted. You see, Jean really was adopted in a sense—so she could have the same last name as everybody else. But she wasn't adopted in the sense that Annette was saying she was, and it bothered Jean. So when Jean started yelling and crying, Annette would laugh and say, "See, you fell for it. You fell for it," even though Jean hadn't fallen for it. It just irritated her to have someone babbling at her like a parrot, saying, "You're adopted. Did you know that? You're adopted. Really, you are. How does it feel?" and following her around and not giving her any peace.

Anyway, that was Annette—a nice girl who had the power to drive everybody crazy.

"Oh, hello," she said when she saw us. "I was just coming up to see how business was doing. I was just reading how little kids who shine shoes in winter often get pneumonia and die."

"I was just reading how kids who read too much on winter afternoons get snow blindness," Jack growled.

"Oh Jack!" she pushed him. "You're so funny! I was just teasing, of course!"

"Oh—a joke!" And he started laughing really hard like he just got it.

"Jack!" I exclaimed. "You be polite. Sorry, Annette. Jack's a grump today, I guess."

The truth was that Jack got grumpy whenever he saw Annette. He just couldn't understand why anyone would go around telling kids that they're adopted. My guess is that they'll marry each other someday.

"Do you know what?" she asked us eagerly. Of course we didn't, so she went right on. "I heard that Scruggs Grady and his gang caught Frank Cairns last night and tried to make him eat a *worm!*"

"What?" I asked. Scruggs Grady and his pals have done some pretty mean things, but that sounded impossible. "Where'd he get a worm in winter?" I asked.

"Oh, his foster dad raises them for bait in his basement," Annette said.

"I bet he steals them!" I mumbled.

"Did Frank eat it?" Jack asked.

"No, after he started crying, they called him a sissy and kept ducking him in the snow. They finally let him go."

"If they weren't sissies themselves, they wouldn't gang up on kids like that," Jack muttered.

"It would be nice if your giant octopus could get ahold of Scruggs and his gang," she said.

"What? You know about our octopus?" Jack demanded.

"Of course I do." And she batted her eyelashes at him as though it were only normal for her to know about such things.

Jack sucked in his breath. "As soon as I find out who told—" he muttered to himself. "Then—the killer octopus will *strike!*"

"What's that?" she asked.

"Nothing—family business."

After we said good-bye to Annette, Jack's face darkened again. "Did you tell her about the octopus?"

"Who cares if I did?" I asked.

"Did you?"

"No, but who cares?" I said again.

"*I* care. The giant killer octopus is for us, the Derwood family."

"You mean you don't like to terrify people who aren't related to you?"

"Stop teasing. I want us to have something at that cabin that nobody anywhere else has."

"We do—fifty tons of snow and an acre and a half of stacked cordwood. I can't think of anybody else who has all that in his back yard, except maybe the Abominable Snowman."

"That's what I mean, Penny. Nobody wants that place. The kids at school think it's funny that I have to go up to the middle of nowhere every weekend and can't play on the hockey team."

"Dad wants us to be closer as a family," I said, defending Dad.

"Right!" He smacked his fist into his hand. "And the octopus has helped us be just that. It's something we've worked at. A family thing. That octopus belongs to Derwood, Incorporated."

"I suppose that you're president of Derwood, Incorporated?"

"Of course not. Dad's president, and Mom's vice-president. I'm the manager in charge of marine life! And as manager, I've made a decision! We need something to remind us that we are Derwoods, and *only* we are Derwoods! The octopus strikes tonight!" And he stalked inside.

FOUR
THE DEATH OF THE OCTOPUS

"Here are the entrepreneurs!" Dad called as I walked in after Jack. "Just in time for a little baby-sitting!"

We looked at each other.

"Your mother and I have to run out and see Mrs. Tucker. She fell and hurt herself this afternoon."

"Is she hurt badly, Dad?" I asked. Mrs. Tucker was elderly, and she ran the Ladies' Auxiliary at church.

"I don't know," he said. "But she has no family nearby, and she needs us. We've already ordered two pizzas for you kids. They'll be delivered in about twenty minutes. Here's the money." He kissed me on top of my head.

"Jack," he said, "make everybody listen to Penny. We should be back before eight. Be good."

Mom came hurrying in from the hallway where she'd been kissing everybody good-bye. Every time Mom and Dad go out for the evening, it takes quite a while for them to get to the door.

"Tell her we'll pray for her," I yelled as they left. They waved, hopped into the car, and drove off. Dad was a deacon, and he always visited church members who were in the hospital.

I realized, of course, that I had been left alone with the kids, Jack, and the giant killer octopus—which at last report from the manager of marine life was loose and on the rampage.

"Jack!"

"What?" he came out holding Marie under one arm. His other hand had Freddy by the collar. "I figured it would be quicker to clean these two if we just threw them in the washer instead of having baths. What do you say?" he asked.

Freddy and Marie were laughing, their breaths coming in short gasps from struggling. They both kicked and squirmed.

"Just as long as they get cleaned," I told him. The little kids liked it when Jack and I teased them. "Could you help me set the table, too?"

"Sure!" He took them to the bathroom to wash their hands. We set the table quickly. Jean poured the colas just as the delivery man came. We got the pizzas served. I passed around plenty of napkins. Pizza, I have found, takes several years to master.

We all liked having a night to ourselves. It made us feel grown-up—that is, everybody except Freddy. He squirmed in his chair and fussed that the food was too hot. Then he cried when Jack joked with him again.

"I can see right now that I'll be the one doing the dishes," Jack said to me. That meant, of course, that I had to run the water for everybody's bath.

I gave Renee and Marie their baths while Freddy fussed and fumed downstairs. In order to keep peace, I got his pajamas for him and his royal blue bathrobe. I rinsed out the tub after my little sisters finished and ran the water for Freddy.

"Come up and take your bath," I called down to him. He swaggered up the stairs—looking like a half-mile of bad road.

He haughtily swept past me and then boldly locked the bathroom door—something he wasn't allowed to do. But I wasn't going to stand on the wrong side of a locked door yelling my head off for him to come out. If I acted like I hadn't noticed, he'd probably get bored and come out.

I had the girls say their praycrs and then put them in bed.

"Tell us a story," Marie begged.

"Tell us an *octopus* story," Renee added.

"Those are Jack's department."

"Please, please," they begged.

"Somebody call me?" Jack asked, walking in.

"Yeah, Jack. It's safe now. Freddy's in the bathroom," I said wryly. Sheepish, he grinned at mc. He was always unloading the hardest baby-sitting jobs on me—like giving baths—but most younger brothers don't help at all, so I couldn't get too mad at him.

"I think," he said, "that it's time for the fifty-ton, mile-long, giant kil-"

"No!" I yelled. "No! Tonight Penny Derwood sleeps by herself! Alone! In the sanctity of her bed, without eight cold hands, eight cold feet, and four pointy right elbows horning in on her beauty sleep! No octopus stories!"

Marie and Renee groaned.

"How about a little one?" Jack asked.

"No!" I was unmovable.

"How about a funny one?" Jack was determined.

"Yeah!" the girls cheered.

"No! No matter how funny you start it, you'll end up scaring them."

Our argument was interrupted by a giant splash from the bathroom.

"Freddy, what are you doing in there boy, surfing?" Jack called.

"He's locked himself in," I mumbled to Jack.

"Hah! Leave it to me. No, wait—" He stopped on his way to the hall. "If I get Freddy to come out in less than one minute, will you let me tell an octopus story?"

"Please, please," the girls begged.

"*Not* a scary one," I said.

"Okay, a funny one," he agreed.

"Okay, you have one minute to get Freddy out."

Jack stepped out into the hallway. Leaning close to the bathroom door, he yelled, "Did you say ice cream, Penny? Have we got ice cream in the freezer?"

There was one last swish of water from inside, and the door popped open. Freddy emerged, soaking wet in his royal blue bathrobe. Jack strategically stuck his foot inside the door.

"Fifteen seconds," he told me.

"What ice cream?" Freddy asked.

"Penny and I were just talking about the ice cream in the freezer," Jack said. "Were you listening?"

Freddy saw he had been tricked and tried to slam the door shut, but he couldn't budge it past Jack's foot.

"Not so fast, buster," Jack said. "Go in there, use a towel to dry off, get your pajamas on, and come out—fast. And don't lock the door."

I was about to challenge Jack on his less-than-honest methods, but the next second I had a new problem.

Freddy looked rebellious.

Jack's eyes narrowed. "Don't forget what came up the drain *before,*" he added.

All signs of rebellion fled. Freddy's eyes got big. He ducked back inside and went to work.

"Jack, you shouldn't scare him like that," I said. This time I kept my foot between the door and the door jam. "He doesn't understand that the octopus isn't real."

"Oh sure he does. Kids love to be scared like that. Don't you remember?"

I frowned at him. "No!"

He grinned and went into the girls' room to tell them a story. "Freddy, that octopus is make-believe," I called through the "foot"-wide crack in the door. I hoped it would help. Freddy wasn't even too sure what make-believe meant.

From my station at the bathroom door I could hear the beginning of Jack's new story in the girls' room and see through the open door into the boys' room. Mom had been sorting the laundry on Freddy's bed. In her hurry, she had left the laundry basket and piles of clean clothes. It looked kind of eerie in the slanted light from the hallway, this big round thing with lumps around it. Maybe it only suggested an octopus to me because I could hear Jack telling his story in the next room. But at night the boys' room always gives me the creeps because, for one thing, Jack's enormous and top-heavy bookcase kind of looms over everything. It almost touches the ceiling. We knocked it over once when we played gorillas on it.

I thought about calling Jean to finish putting the clothes away while I guarded the bathroom door, but she was downstairs working on her fourth-grade bug

collection. Fourth grade was proving to be a hard year for her. It had been hard for me, too, because when I was in fourth grade, I was too scared to touch bugs.

I was the only kid in the school to make a bug collection without touching a single one—not even a wing. I captured them all with Jack's catcher's mitt and his baseball glove. At first a lot of them got squashed, but I learned. After that I got to play third base on the girls' softball team. Education really pays off. But when Jack found out what I'd been doing with his mitt and glove, he made me learn to touch bugs. It used to give me the shivers, but I had to learn. He taught me by leaving them everywhere, even in my bed.

I decided to let Jean keep working on her bugs and put the clothes away myself later. I could hear snatches of Jack's story from the next room. He was making burbling noises like the octopus was coming up a drain somewhere.

And then Freddy cautiously emerged from the bathroom. He paused at the doorway to the girls' room. But when he heard the word *octopus,* he hurried on. Poor kid.

I was about to tell him he'd have to wait while I cleared his bed, but Freddy didn't give me a chance. He was staring at his bed, and next thing I knew, he'd launched himself against the bookcase, trying to tip it over.

"Freddy!" I screamed. I ran in and snatched him back, but it was too late.

Jack and the girls heard me scream, and they came out to see what was wrong. The tall bookcase wavered from the push it had received. The topmost books plopped gracefully to the floor, and then the whole thing fell forward with a crash. Right across the bed.

"Oh no," Jack groaned.

As if in agreement, the bed suddenly broke.

"It was the giant killer octopus!" Freddy gasped. "And I didn't have any sugar!"

From downstairs we heard the front door open. "Kids? Anybody home?"

It never fails. Things can go well for two solid hours, and the *one* minute when everything falls apart is the same minute that Mom and Dad walk through the door. I could hear them coming up the stairs.

"The octopus was on the bed, waiting to catch me!" Freddy exclaimed.

"My hands have that itchy feeling that tells me I'm going to be holding a snow shovel soon," Jack said.

We started clearing loose books off the broken bed. That was when Mom and Dad walked in, laughing with each other and chatting. Our dogged silence greeted them.

"What?" Dad exclaimed.

Freddy burst out crying and ran to Mom.

"What happened?" Mom asked. "You weren't playing gorillas on the bookcase again, were you?"

"Jack," Dad began. "What did you do to—"

"Nothing, Dad, honest!" Jack exclaimed.

Dad lent a hand with righting the bookcase. As we lifted it off, amid a shower of falling books, Renee yelled, "It was the clothes basket!"

What had once been Mom's clothes basket was now a flattened pancake on the broken bed.

"I thought it was a octopus," Freddy confessed.

"*An* octopus, dear," Mom corrected.

"I pushed the bookcase onto it."

Dad sighed and looked at the wrecked bed. Then he looked at the ceiling, as though trying to count up how many cars this was worth. Jack and I held our breath, hoping he would decide we weren't at fault.

"Penny and Jack," he said at last. "Come downstairs."

"I knew it," Jack said to me as we walked downstairs. "I just knew that somehow, some way, all of this was going to be *our* fault."

"I have some terrible news," Dad said when we followed him into the living room.

"What's that, Dad?" I asked.

He turned to the wall, his hands behind his back. "Terrible news," he repeated gravely. He turned around, his head down, his eyes serious.

"The fifty-ton, mile-long, giant killer octopus was run over by an aircraft carrier today," he said.

Jack and I looked at each other uneasily.

"It was?" Jack asked at last.

"Oh my, hadn't you heard? Yes, it was. Killed instantly. But scientists say it never felt a thing, so you can rest easy about that. It has now been stuffed and put on display at the Smithsonian Institution."

Jack and I looked at each other again.

"Do you know what this means?" Dad asked.

"What?"

"The reign of the giant killer octopus is now ended. It is no more, kaput, finished. And do you know what else that means?"

"What?" we asked.

"If I hear one more story about the fifty-ton, mile-long, giant killer octopus, two of my children will be shoveling the snow off Lake Michigan and all its beaches. Do I make myself clear?"

"Yes, Dad."

"Jack, Freddy is scared out of his wits and bedless. Your bed is big enough to share for a few nights."

"Yes, sir."

I shouldn't have, but I couldn't help bending forward and laughing just then. It felt so good to know that Jack finally had to sleep with one of the kids. I caught myself when I saw Dad looking at me, but then when I saw he wasn't mad, I leaned over and laughed really hard.

"What are you laughing at?" Jack demanded.

I straightened up. "Private joke."

"Between you and Dad?"

"Between me and myself."

Jack looked like he thought I was crazy.

Dad sighed. "We'll have to get your brother a new bed. I suppose we won't be able to go up to the cabin this weekend."

A light was dawning on Jack's face. "Say, maybe Penny and I can find a good deal at that mattress place across from the quick mart."

"Uh-huh, and you two detectives can take a look around, huh?"

"Well, it crossed my mind."

"You can get some prices on box springs there, but I think you'll find the place to be just a run-down mattress store. Criminals don't hide out in places like that any more."

Boy, was *he* going to find out differently!

FIVE

IN SEARCH OF AMY BELLE

The next afternoon Jack and I asked Mr. Scott if we could leave our shoe-shine stuff outside the store while we looked at box springs.

"Ah!" Mr. Scott said with a knowing wink. "Doing a little detective work over at the hide-out, eh?"

I just smiled as we left, but Jack looked crushed. "How'd he know?" he asked as we crossed the street. "I thought I'd been hiding it so well. First Dad figures out that we're watching the store—even Mr. Scott figures it out. Why? I thought I was pretty good at being secretive and mysterious."

"You're about as secretive as a pane of glass," I told him. He didn't like my joke. But we were both quiet as I pushed open the door of the mattress store, and we walked in, Jack trailing me at my elbow.

It looked as dingy inside as it did out. One long sheet of cardboard—the length and width of a single mattress—hung from the ceiling. One side of it had mattress lengths marked on it. The other side had another picture of the cartoon mattress-man, holding his candle and yawning. There were different piles of mattresses stacked by twos around the store, some lying flat and some on their sides. It would have been a great place to build a fort. Overhead, a huge, dirty fan hung down from the ceiling, lazily flinging bits of dust and dirt off its great blades. The place really did remind me of that creepy textile factory.

"Sinister," I whispered. "This place looks too much like a hide-out to be a hide-out. What do you think?" But Jack didn't answer. I was about to nudge him when a man at the other end of the narrow room looked up. He was slouched over a counter, reading a paper. He had a bald head and big belly.

"What do you want, kid?" he growled.

I put on my grown-up voice. "We came to price box springs."

"Get lost. You came in to get warm. No loitering."

My grown-up voice would obviously have to be perfected at a later date. "We didn't come in to get warm," I said. "We came to look at box springs. My little brother broke his bed last night and—"

The guy stood up. "No lip, kid. I'm a busy man. Get out."

"But—"

He started to walk toward me. "Go on, hit the road."

I turned to Jack—who I thought had been awfully quiet for Jack—and found that he wasn't there. "Hey!" But I caught myself at the sight of a leather shoe disappearing under one of the bare beds.

"Scat!" the man exclaimed at me. I decided not to argue.

"Okay, okay, I'm going. But you're going to be sorry when you find out I really was looking for a box spring." And I walked out, feeling uncommonly dumb.

I stalked back to the quick mart and set up the shoe-shine kit. Nothing to do, I figured, but wait for Jack.

The minutes ticked by. He was probably having all sorts of adventures—finding a hidden laboratory down below or all sorts of important people kidnaped and tied up, waiting to be shipped out to other countries and held for ransom. I read a story once about a kidnaper who knocked his victims out and coated them with wax so that they looked like wax dummies of themselves. Then he sneaked past all sorts of police and detectives with these wax dummies of famous people and put them up in his wax museum. He told people he wanted to keep a collection of wax statues of the people who had just disappeared—that way interest would stay high in his wax museum. And nobody knew he really had those people hidden away and unconscious in the statues of themselves.

Then one day his air conditioning broke, and his building got really hot. So he tried to shoo everybody out before the wax all melted away. And wouldn't you know it, some twelve-year-old girl figured out why he was so scared, and she hid while everybody else left. Then she explored around and saw some of the statues melt away and show the people under them, asleep and tied up stiff against poles. She called the police and got a big reward and shook hands with the president and went to Taiwan to have another adventure. That was in the first book in the Amy Belle series.

I sat there thinking what I would do if I went into the basement and saw a bunch of wax dummies down there. I would know what to do right away. I would turn the heat up in the building to melt the wax. Then I'd set them free, and I'd get to meet the president, too.

Just like Amy Belle, the girl detective. If I got to be just like Amy Belle, I wouldn't mind—not a bit.

I sort of jumped when a customer stomped his foot down on the box in front of me, and for a minute I didn't know what he was doing. Then I remembered that I was manning the shoe-shine kit as part of our front, and I went to work, but I couldn't make the rag snap and crack like Jack could, and there was no way I was going to try any new accents while I worked. I finished up, and the man paid me, but he didn't give me a tip.

More minutes ticked by. Maybe the bald man with the bulging stomach had caught Jack and was putting him to the test. That had happened to Amy Belle, too. These crooks had left her to starve in this old shack,

but two cowboys passing by on their way to a local rodeo had stopped to get out of the rain. They set her free, and one of them nearly fell in love with her when he found out how brave and fearless and honest and good-natured she was. But she wouldn't have him, although she was very much obliged, I'm sure. Even though she was only twelve, she was engaged to Phil Philmont back in her hometown of Cranberry Heights. That was in the book, *Amy Belle and the Mystery in Abilene.* It's the fifth book in the Amy Belle series.

Mr. Scott came out of the store armed with a squirt bottle of window cleaner. He started to wash the front windows of the quick mart—a sure sign that supper time was approaching. "Where's your Hungarian brother?" he asked.

"Over at the mattress store." Which was true enough. He was probably being put to the test even as we were talking, and there I was with a shoe-shine rag in my hand. Seemed like I should have thought of something brilliant and convinced Mr. Scott to help me—that's what Amy Belle does when she's in a jam—but I didn't think of anything, and Mr. Scott just went on wiping the glass.

"Ah! Your brother is doing his detecting, eh?"

"Yes, he sure is." And probably being coated with wax right now, I added to myself. I wondered if the blowtorch back at the house would help.

Mr. Scott finished his windows and went back inside.

More time dragged on. I began to hope that Jack really was in danger, because if we were late for dinner, we were going to get in trouble. It would be nice to have a good excuse like, "Two kidnapers were dipping me in wax, and I was unconscious at the time."

I realized that it was getting dark. Two great banks of dim clouds were on either side of the sky, and as the sun set, their shadows lengthened, reaching crosswise and lengthwise like slow fingers on a giant hand, spreading out to each other. When those fingers met, it would be dark. I felt nervous. Where was Jack?

I closed up the shoe-shine kit and waited. Mr. Scott had gone home for his supper. One of the other cashiers was running the store.

I could see one streetlight from where I sat. It slowly glowed brighter—first with a watery, waning light that was almost pink, then with the familiar white glare as twilight deepened. I glanced across the street at the mattress store and realized that it was closed. They really had kidnaped my brother! "Jack!" I whispered.

An answer boomed in my ear. "Yeah?"

His voice, loud in the quietness, almost sent me through the awning overhead. "Yagh!" I yelled, and jumped. Then I turned to see him, perfectly safe, brushing dust off his coat sleeve. I gaped at him.

"Calm down, Penny. It's just me."

"Jack, how did you get out of there?" I tried not to let on how scared I had been. "What took you so long?"

He looked embarrassed. "I—uh—got locked in a closet."

"They locked you in a closet?"

"N-no. I-I locked myself in there by accident." He was gathering up our shoe-shine stuff, trying to act calm.

"You've been in that store two hours. Do you mean you spent two hours in a closet?"

"Course not. I'm not that foolish. I only spent an hour and forty-five minutes in the closet. The first five minutes and the last ten minutes I was as free as a bird. Come on." He took the shoe-shine kit from me. "Are we ever going to catch it from Dad."

"I'll say," I agreed. "Somewhere in this town there are two snow shovels with our names on them."

"What else could go wrong?" Jack was hurrying now.

"We never found out how much box springs cost."

"Agh!" He winced and then glared at me. "Did you have to say that?"

"Sorry," I said.

"Well," he sighed and looked resigned. "At least nothing else can go wrong."

I grabbed his arm. "Jack!"

He moaned and put his face in his hands. "Why do I say things like that?"

"Do you see him?" I whispered.

"Yes. He and two or three others are behind the hedge up there."

"It's Scruggs," I whimpered. I decided right then that I didn't really want to be like Amy Belle.

"Don't stop walking—they'll just catch us anyway," he said.

Something glittered in the faint glow from the streetlights.

"Penny." Jack slipped his gloved hand over mine. "He's carrying a can of worms."

SIX

THE AMY BELLE STYLE

"What do we do, walk into their trap?" I whispered. By now Scruggs must have seen that we knew he was waiting for us.

"I have a confession to make," Jack said suddenly, whispering. "I-I read one of those detective books of yours once—an Amy Belle book."

"You did?" For a moment I even forgot Scruggs. I wanted to ask Jack if he'd liked it, but then he said, "Yeah. I read *Amy Belle and the Moon Surface Oil Rig Caper.* Do you remember what happens on page 38?"

"Of course not."

"You know!" his voice was urgent. We were almost even with Scruggs, who would doubtless have some of his friends close in behind us. "Remember what Amy Belle did when those enemy agents had her and her chums Muffy and Flip trapped next to the tank of rocket fuel?"

"Yeah—oh, no Jack. No, I couldn't. Not that—" I begged.

(For those who haven't read *Amy Belle and the Moon Surface Oil Rig Caper,* Amy pretended to stoop down and tie her shoe right behind the thugs just as Muffy and Flip pushed them backwards. The bad guys fell heels over head—disastrous on a low-gravity surface like the moon's—and all the girls got away while the men were bouncing around trying to get on their feet again.) "It's the last chance we have!"

"I can't! I decided I don't want to be like Amy Belle. I—"

"If it works, I'll give you five dollars!"

"Five dollars! Okay." For five dollars I would act like King Kong if Jack asked me to.

I bent down and untied my boot lace. The plan was for me to say my boot was untied, and then sort of stoop behind Scruggs to tie it. Then Jack would butt into Scruggs, who—hopefully—would topple backwards over me and into one or both the others while we took advantage of the distraction and escaped.

Just as I was untying one of them, Scruggs and two of his cronies came rushing at us from three directions. My heart sank. Scruggs alone seemed tough enough, although he never threatened anybody when he was by himself, but now it was Scruggs plus two others.

The two others circled us like they thought we might try to get away, but Jack just stood there, his body relaxed and yet poised, as though ready to do anything—except fight. He kept his eyes on Scruggs.

"Hi, Scruggs."

"Hiya, Jack." Scruggs knocked Jack's hat off.

"How's the Society for the Prevention of Cruelty to Thugs doing?" Jack asked.

"What'sat?" Scruggs asked casually, taking the shoe-shine box out of Jack's hand. He opened it up. "Why, isn't this nice? A shoe-shine kit! I think I'll borrow it. My shoes could use some shining."

The two others came and stood behind Scruggs. They knew we weren't going anyplace. They stood there in a group, leering at us.

"Scruggs, you don't need your shoes polished. I thought kids like you just swung from tree to tree," Jack said. I caught my breath. Jack was treading on mighty thin ice, saying stuff like that to Scruggs. Scruggs grabbed Jack by the front of his jacket. "You being funny, Derwood?"

"Oh no, Scruggs. I didn't mean it! Say, why don't I shine your boots, Scruggs? Please? I got lots of black polish."

I glared at Jack. What was he begging for?

Scruggs and his friends laughed.

"Just don't hit me, Scruggs. You wouldn't hit a little kid, would you?" Jack asked. "And you wouldn't make him eat a worm, would you?"

Scruggs swung the shoe-shine kit back into Jack's hand. "Go on, shine my boots." Then I knew what Jack had been doing. Scruggs had to lift one foot onto the box. It would make the bully off balance. I got ready to bend down and tie my boot so that Jack could push him over me, but one of the others interrupted me. "Hey, girl!" he said.

I glanced around. "Me?" I asked.

"Yeah," he said. "*You* shine *my* boots. Now."

"Um—I need a box," I said softly.

He laughed. He picked up his big boot and rested it on Jack's back as Jack was bent over on the snow. "This'll do. Start shining." That was the end of the Amy Belle plan.

Jack handed the polish up to me, and a rag. He looked pretty scared. Not long from now we would both be eating worms for dinner. But suddenly the rag gave me an idea.

"Uh, we like to act Hungarian," I said quietly as I put the waxy polish on the dirty boot. "It gives us a better—incentive, I guess you might say, to shine shoes that way."

Jack must have been astonished, knowing how I hated pretending to be Hungarian in front of people, but he didn't look up. Maybe he knew I was working out a plan.

"It does, huh?"

"S-sometimes Jack sings." That was true. "But I don't sing." That was also true.

"Oh, yeah? Well, you sing. Now. In Hungarian."

"Do I have to?"

He raised his voice. "Do it!"

I cleared my voice and started singing—really quietly. Of course they started laughing and smirking right away, so they didn't know what I was saying, but I hoped Jack was listening to me—to my words.

> "Grabski rag,
> Grabski rag,
> Pullski 'round the bootski.
> Over on the ice-ovitch,
> Throw him by his bootski."

While I was singing, Jack quickly wrapped his rag around the back of Scruggs' heel and grabbed either end as I did the same with my rag.

"Now, Jack!" We both pulled with quick, hard jerks. Scruggs flew backward into the third fellow. They both hit the snowy street. The one I threw stumbled but didn't fall. We didn't wait around to watch. Jack grabbed the money sack out of the kit, and we both ran, leaving our box and stool behind.

We cut through the yards of some houses, hoping we wouldn't find any fences. Some of the people had been snow-blowing their driveways clear since the first snow, and welcome drifts were piled high all along the sidewalks. We climbed over these and slid down them. I thought my lungs would burst from moving so fast in such heavy clothing, but I managed to keep up with Jack. The drifts, we hoped, would lose us from sight.

"Suicide Hill," Jack gasped. "Step on it!"

Suicide Hill is called Springman's Hill eight months of the year, but in the winter it takes on a more sinister reputation. Kids hose it down in early winter, and they keep hosing it down through all the freezes to keep it the fastest sledding hill in Peabody.

We shinnied down Suicide Hill—almost breaking our necks, and then we finally found a highway with houses backed up along it. A deep, snowy gully ran between the back yards and the edge of the cleared highway. The gully had high ridges of snow on either side of it. We struggled through this gully the rest of the way, losing the bullies once and for all, and eventually making our way back to our neighborhood, with its familiar, cheerful streetlights and the houses we knew so well.

We trampled down some loose snow as we forced a way through two back yards, and then we walked easily up the plowed street with its hard-packed and dirty covering, and up our rutted driveway. Only then did we realize how late we were. Jack's wristwatch read 8:00. Without a word—he was too tired—he slipped his gloved hand over mine, and we went inside.

Dad was on the phone talking urgently to the parents of one of our friends. Mom came out of the kitchen just in time to see us walk in.

"Where have you been?" she demanded, half-stern and half-frightened.

"Running away from three big kids."

"Who?"

"Scruggs Grady and two of his friends."

Dad heard our voices and came out. He looked ready to be angry, but I think he was too glad to see us to not give us a chance to explain.

"Well?" he asked.

I pulled off my scarf and looked down. I was still clutching one end of the rag in my mittened hand. Both my hands were shaking when I took off my mittens. Jack explained what happened with Scruggs while I took off my coat and sat down. I still felt scared inside. I suppose it was normal for Mom and Dad to want an explanation right away, but I kind of wished they would have just given us dinner first and let us rest. And I really felt entitled to some special attention, after having slain three giants with my brother, and us armed only with slings. Not even real slings—rags converted to slings.

"I'm going to find out who that boy's parents are," Dad said. "Somebody's got to tell them what their son is doing. Carrying a can of worms like that—how cruel! How can he do that to children?"

He went into the kitchen for the telephone, while Mom went to warm up some dinner for us. Unexpectedly I felt a kiss on top of my head. I looked up.

"If you ever tell anyone I did that, they wouldn't believe you," Jack said, laughing. "I owe you five dollars."

"I never did bend down behind Scruggs to trip him. That's what Amy Belle did," I admitted. I would have let Jack off the five dollars anyway. His plan had been a good one; I had just modified it to fit the situation.

"You've outdone Amy Belle."

After Mom and Dad calmed down and Dad couldn't find out how to reach Scruggs's house, they both sat with us while we ate and told us about all the places they thought we had been. Dad told us about the bullies that used to pick on him, and how he had tried to outwit them. The best way of outwitting them, he had found, was by having his two older brothers go everywhere with him.

"I don't have that option," Jack replied mildly. "My only older brother is my sister."

"She did pretty well for herself this time," Dad added.

"I had an older sister who was better than any older brother too." Mom started to laugh, then remembered how mad she was at Scruggs Grady.

"Still, we should do something about that boy— imagine, being a teenager and enjoying himself by hurting others!" Mom said. "You should warn him next time—if there is a next time—that your parents will have him punished."

"Mom, he would laugh in our faces, and pretty soon it would get all over the neighborhood," I said gently. "Scruggs's parents never punish him. Why should he be scared of you and Dad?"

She sighed and gave in. "I wonder why they never punish him."

"Maybe they don't love him," Jack said simply, and then he didn't say anything else.

Dad raised an eyebrow and looked at Jack a little strangely. I had the idea that he had just said something impressive, but I couldn't figure out what it was.

"Well," Dad said at last. "I suppose that next time you two are late for dinner we can call the police and have them escort you home."

"Well, really," I said, looking guiltily at Jack. "We were already ten minutes late when we started home. You see, we went into the mattress store and—"

"Ten minutes late is not nearly as alarming as two hours late," Dad said, smiling. "I think I can forgive the ten minutes."

And he didn't ask anything else.

It was okay with me not to tell him how silly we'd been—me getting kicked out right away and Jack locking himself in a closet.

As far as I was concerned, the mystery was over. It wasn't until much later, after I'd taken a hot bath and was getting up from my prayers, that Jack knocked on my open door. He had his robe on, too, and was ready for bed. Jean was already asleep, so Jack and I had to keep our voices down.

"I got a secret," he said, "about an adventure."

"Jack, I've hung up my holsters and my Amy Belle novels," I told him. "No new adventures for Penny Derwood. She's become manager of peacetime activities in Derwood, Incorporated."

"No problem," he said. "This is not a *new* adventure. It's an old one."

"Scruggs?" I asked.

"No, not Scruggs. Scruggs is one of the complications that any good detective runs into—"

"Oh yes. Even Amy Belle has one of those: In *Amy Belle and the Secret in Turkey* some kid up the street was always letting the air out of the tires of her jaunty little convertible—just when she needed it for a getaway."

"Yeah, yeah." He waved it away impatiently. "Forget Amy Belle right now. Forget Scruggs, too. I'm talking about the mattress company."

I felt my jaw drop. "What mystery? You sat in there for two hours and didn't hear anything."

He looked startled. "Who told you I didn't hear anything? I never said I didn't hear anything."

"Well . . . no. You never said you didn't, but I figured you would have told me right away if you had."

"Ah!" He leaned against the door frame. "No, I kept quiet for once. I seriously considered taking this case myself, Watson. So I almost didn't tell you—"

"No fair!" Then I hurriedly looked at Jean to make sure I hadn't wakened her up.

He threw his hands into the air. "Twenty seconds ago you had hung up your holsters. Now all of a sudden you're back on the trail," he whispered, stepping into the room.

"Okay. I'm back on the trail. If you're in on something, I'm in on it too."

He grinned, drew an imaginary six-shooter, flipped it around in his hand, and then tossed it to me. I caught it and holstered it in an imaginary holster.

"Not bad, pardner," he said. "After you saved my skin tonight, I figured I'd tell you everything. Anybody who can sing a Hungarian folk song to the tune of 'Jingle Bells' has got to be my partner."

I wasn't satisfied by his charm. "Look here, Jack, sitting on a freezing cold curb in the middle of January makes me your partner. It's not fair to keep secrets!"

He held out his hand to shake. "Okay, I'm sorry. You're right; no more secrets—you're my partner." We shook hands, and he sat down next to me.

"So what did you hear?" I asked him.

"Wonderful things. The closet was right by the counter where the grumpy guy was standing, and behind the counter there's a back room. There were two other guys back there talking. First I was going to yell and bang and ask them to let me out. But then when I heard what they were saying, I figured it would be safer to keep quiet."

"What were they saying?"

"All this stuff about getting shipments out on time and dropping off a person named Moses. They kept on shushing each other the whole two hours and looking out for any customers. That's what the guy at the counter was doing—sort of a look-out, you know?"

"Sounds to me like they were just concerned about making a buck."

"No, Penny. They're shipping their mattresses to Alaska. Do you know what is up there?"

"What?"

"Russia."

"Really? Russia's up in Alaska? Doesn't that mean we own it?"

"No! If I knew as little about geography as you, I wouldn't let myself be seen in public, Penny Derwood."

"You could only do that if you were invisible. And you're the one who said Russia is in Alaska, not me. What did you mean by it?"

"Russia's up there—just past Alaska—separated by a narrow strip of ocean and ice. About fifty miles, I think."

"I never knew that!"

"If those mugs wanted to smuggle something out of this country to Russia, that would be the way to go—through Alaska," he told me. "What could they be smuggling in something as flat as mattresses, I wonder."

"Ironing boards, maybe?" I asked.

"No! Quit making jokes!" He sighed and looked annoyed. He was serious. "I couldn't catch everything they said, but they kept calling something their stash and their stuff. They wouldn't use the real name. And there's some other guy—a sort of manager of smuggling, I suppose, who they're planning to meet somewhere with the stuff. They called him Tom Thumb. He's in charge of getting the mattresses and the Moses guy onto the right freight train."

His words jolted me. "It's not a game, then. There is something that they're putting in the mattresses. And that Moses might be a spy they're planting."

"That's what I've been telling you. Did you really think that a two-bit mattress place would be doing regular business with stores in Alaska? No way!"

"We should tell Mom and Dad." I wasn't feeling as brave as Amy Belle at this point.

"We can't!" he explained. "They would just laugh at us. They haven't taken us seriously about this, yet."

"Well . . ." I felt bad because I'd been kind of laughing at Jack, too, just going along with him for something to do.

"No," he said. "They're going to be taking a shipment somewhere tomorrow night. All we have to do is get one mattress, Penny, and get it over to Sergeant McKenna's house. Then we can tell the whole story."

"And then just rest on our laurels, huh?"

"Sure, if you've got some."

"How are we going to get a mattress, anyway?"

"Capture one. How else?"

"But—isn't that stealing?"

"No, it's not stealing! Is it stealing when police raid a place and take everything for evidence? You and I are doing our duty as Americans if those mugs are smuggling something to a foreign country."

"Okay. How are we going to *capture* a mattress and get it to the police in time?"

"Easy. We take it straight to Sergeant McKenna's, for one thing, because he tipped us off in the first place, so I want him to get his share of the fame and reward. Tomorrow afternoon we'll slip behind the mattress place. There's a hill just above the loading area there."

"Yeah?"

"Well, first, before they start loading, we're going to set up trash cans at the top of the hill."

"Okay."

"We hide behind the trash cans when they start loading. They go back inside for another load, and we sneak to the far side of the building, right behind where they'll be putting the mattresses into the truck, so we can peek around the corner and see them."

"Okay so far."

"Then when they go in for another load, you close and bar the loading dock door, and I'll start pulling out as small a mattress as I can find. Then we run like fury to Sergeant McKenna's house—way ahead of the thugs. They won't even know what direction we left in—because they'll try to get the back door open and then have to run all the way to the front and back around. By that time we'll be cutting through yards to the Sergeant's house. Easy as pie. Once we get there, I open up the mattress and—presto! Out drops money, jewels, paintings, or whatever those guys are smuggling. You and I go find a box of laurels somewhere and rest on them."

He stood up, satisfied. "Boy, and then we can hang up our holsters."

"Or be hung in our turn." I was skeptical.

He shook his head. "Nothing can go wrong. I'm sure."

"Statements like that were made about the *Titanic,* too."

SEVEN

BEYOND THE AMY BELLE STYLE

Morning came—a clear, crisp morning that gives a person hope for spring. The air was cold, but the sky looked like it was washed and ready. Some of the snow melted during the midday, but in the afternoon the temperature dropped, and everything began freezing again as though late February intended to hold on to the bitter end. We walked home from school over a slick and shining world that had lost much of its beauty to us. I was hungry for spring.

"Boots for sure," Jack said as we trudged home. "It won't be easy carrying that thing all that way."

In the dim night before, when the house was quiet, Jack had been bold and sure about his plan. Now in the glare of the cold day, with people everywhere to see us, I think he was a little less confident, but he wouldn't admit it. Not even to himself.

"Jack, are you absolutely *sure* they're smugglers?"

"Yes."

"Tell me again how you're sure."

"The guys said they've got a truckload of mattresses with 'the stuff' all ready to go. They plan to meet Tom Thumb at the second drop-off place. Tom Thumb will pay them and supervise getting the mattresses and a fake invoice into a freight car bound ultimately for Juneau. Now that's everything I remember, all in a nutshell. I couldn't take notes locked up in a closet like I was."

"I wonder who Tom Thumb really is?" I said.

"I don't know—they seemed kind of scared of him. Every time they mentioned him, their voices got really low, so I couldn't make out much of what they said."

"Probably he's some big bald guy with a bearskin coat and a handlebar mustache."

He shrugged. "We don't have to worry about him— just get that one mattress for evidence and be heroes by dinnertime. The police in Alaska can intercept the mattresses and that mug with the code name of Moses. I think they're sending him up there, too."

The thought of being a hero made me smile. Heroes. Kids like Scruggs Grady would be begging for my autograph soon.

But at the thought of Scruggs my smile must have turned into a wince. Just that morning Jack and I had returned to the scene of last night's adventure. The wooden shoe-shine kit and folding stool had been smashed to flinders, and frozen blotches of red, brown, and black were all that was left of the cans of polish.

"A loss," Jack had said automatically, meaning a financial loss. He had surveyed the wreckage calmly, his hands thrust deep into his parka. At last he had merely added, "We probably took a loss on about half of our investment." Then he had lifted his head, his hair, faintly red in the morning light, stirred up a little in the wind. "Come on." And he had walked away, not looking back at the mess. For a moment I had stood helplessly watching him, but then I followed. It would have done no good to rant and rave. Jack never did things like that when he was truly angry; I copied him. In my heart—and in his heart—a grudge began to grow against Scruggs Grady.

We changed to grubbier clothes when we got home, and we put our oldest and sturdiest pairs of boots on. Mom knew we usually went up to the quick mart in the afternoons. But if something went wrong today— well, I could just see myself tied up and gagged and lying on a pile of mattresses in a freight train bound for Juneau, riding along with this guy Moses keeping an eye on me.

But Jack—permanently an optimist—chattered on and on as we walked up our street and the next street and cut across the slick field to the quick mart.

Cutting through the field was our usual route when there was still daylight. The field backed up on the quick mart. Halfway across, Jack led me along so that we kept the store between us and the highway. We cut behind some houses, crossed the highway further up a short way, and came in toward the mattress store from the back.

We came in along the side of the office building. It was situated atop the hill Jack had mentioned earlier. We set up four trash cans and hid behind them while we watched the back of the mattress store below us. No truck was in sight.

We crouched back there, waiting and waiting. I couldn't take it very long and scrunched down to a sitting position. But when I did that, I hit one of the metal trash cans with my knee and knocked it over. It careened over and went rolling down the small hill toward the

mattress store, making a loud clanging as it bumped on the icy asphalt.

"Penny," Jack hissed. "Be careful! You'll blow our cover!"

He looked around to make sure all was clear, then scuttled down the hill and retrieved the can, stuffing the trash back into it and cramping its lid back on. He lugged it back up that dangerously gleaming hill and set it back in place in front of me. "Now be careful!" he hissed. But he wasn't looking where he was going when he stepped back from the cans. His foot slipped on the sloping asphalt behind him, and he flung out his hand to grab hold of something—anything. Anything turned out to be another trash can. It did a neat flipover, somehow keeping its lid on, and—*bumpity, bumpity, bumpity*—rolled down the hill toward the loading zone.

He glared at me like it was *my* fault. "You get this one," he whispered.

I sighed and scrambled down the steep hill, scurrying from one sanded patch to another. This trash can must have been a lot heavier than the first one. I had to pull it by both handles and kind of drag it along, walking backwards up the hill as carefully as I could. But when I got to the steepest part—also the iciest part—I pulled too hard on the unyielding handles and slipped so that I sat down, really hard, and the trash can fell on top of me with a clang and a thud. I saw stars, but through the stars I could hear *bumpity, bumpity, bumpity* as it started to roll away again.

"No you don't!" I yelled, and flung myself on top of it. It rolled over one time with me on top of it and then under it, then stopped. But we were stuck—the trash can and I—because I couldn't sit up with it, it being too heavy and the ground being a sheet of ice. And if I let go of either handle to pull myself up, I knew it would slide away from me and get out of my grasp. The hill was too steep and the can too heavy for me to move.

At that moment I heard Jack's hoarse and frantic whisper. "Penny, get up here. Get up here. Do you hear me?"

Of course I could hear him, but I had landed, clutching the trash can with two hands and two heels, with my back to him. I couldn't turn around to talk to him, and I didn't dare shout.

"Get up here! What are you doing lying down! Get up here!" he hissed.

"I-I can't." I whispered it as loudly as I could, but of course he couldn't hear me because I was talking into the trash can.

"Penny!"

"I said I can't!" I whispered again. At last he must have figured out I was having some problems, because I heard him easing down after me.

"I got it," he said. "Let go." What he didn't tell me was that he'd only gotten hold of the handle on the lid. He didn't realize what I could have told him—the trash can was too heavy to hold by the lid, no matter how hard it had been pushed on. As soon as I let go, the trash can slid sideways and pulled free of the lid in his hand.

Bumpity, bumpity, bumpity. Down it went, with clumps of trash rolling freely out of its mouth. Jack looked down at me. "Just go hide," he growled. "I'll get the trash can."

He managed to retrieve it and stuff it full again with trash. Then he lugged it back up the hill and set it up again as part of our barricade. After he resumed his place with me behind the trash cans, I was more careful. But soon I began to feel cold . . . and bored. I tried not to fidget, but our hiding place was pretty miserable.

The cold came seeping through my clothes. "I'm cold," I said after exactly one hour had passed.

"Me too."

"Really cold."

He knew I was hinting at hot chocolate. We could run over to the quick mart and be back in less than ten minutes. I pointed this fact out to him.

"Penny, in less than ten minutes we can destroy our chances of becoming heroes."

"How? We could always sneak back."

"They'd see us."

I sighed an irritated and grumpy sigh. What did Amy Belle see in this line of work? Anybody who thinks school or anything else is boring should try hiding behind four overstuffed and tipsy trash cans for an entire afternoon in the dead of winter. But, as I thought about it, I realized that Amy Belle never did *this* sort of sleuthing. Clues just always happened to hop across her path.

"Say," I whispered. "I wonder if those Amy Belle novels are as realistic as they try to come off."

"You don't want to be like her anymore anyway, do you?" he asked.

"I do if it would get me out from behind these trash cans," I grumbled.

"Quit complaining."

"I don't like this."

"We're partners," Jack said. He could hear a truck on the highway, and he was craning his neck to see if it was pulling in. But dozens of trucks had passed on the highway. I wasn't interested in this one.

"If we're partners, then we should do what *I* want to do every now and then."

"Last night you were begging me to let you in on this," he said.

"I wasn't numb with cold, then. I—"

"Shhh! Look!" He pointed down to a big truck that was pulling into the tiny loading zone below us. I don't know if it was his shoulder or my shoulder or just our movement, but something knocked over one of the cans just as he pointed. It gave a tired groan of rusted metal and slowly toppled over—*bumpity, bumpity, bumpity.*

Jack grabbed me and pushed us both behind the other three cans. Even if the driver of the truck had looked up, he must not have seen us.

We waited until he went inside to get his cohorts. Jack's hands were still clutching my arm, and I could feel how tense he was. In another minute or so two more men came out—one I recognized from the day before. They had a forklift loaded with mattresses. They lifted mattress after mattress into the truck, each mattress covered in its own box or at least in heavy plastic wrapping.

At last they went inside to get another load. Jack and I hurried down the hill and hid around the corner of the building. By peeking a little, we could see into the big truck, which was much less than half full of mattresses.

The men came out, groaning and complaining about the weight of the mattresses, the poor quality of their forklift, and the severity of the weather for a job like this. I could hardly bear being within ten feet of them, as yet unnoticed but so vulnerable. They needed only to have grabbed us there in that desolate alley and nobody would have known. It would be a cold ride to Juneau.

But the men never suspected we were there. At last they went to get more mattresses. I slipped around the corner to the big sliding door, got behind it, and pushed. At first it didn't budge; then at last it gave. I threw it forward, and it closed with a snap. Instantly I slammed the bolt home and pushed down a catch to lock it. Then I ran to help Jack, who was sliding one of the children's single bed mattresses out of its box.

We heard them pounding angrily on the door, and then events took an unexpected turn.

We had expected the men to run all the way to the front of the store and around the building. Instead, a gloved fist smashed through a back window.

"They're climbing out!" I yelled.

Jack finally got the wide, flat mattress hoisted down to me. I got hold of one end as best as I could. He jumped down with his end and yelled, "Run! After me!"

The mattress had cloth handles sewn into it. As we stumbled past the truck and up the hill, I managed to work my hands into two of these. Jack seemed to have a good grip on the front, but he was running awkwardly, sort of sideways.

"We're going the wrong way to get to McKenna's!" I yelled.

"We'll cut around—lose 'em the same way we lost Scruggs!" he shouted back, panting.

Clumsily, we got up the slick hill. As we rushed past the trash cans, I gave them a hard kick, and they clattered down the hill. I risked a look back at our pursuers and saw them dodging the cans this way and that on the slippery hill, getting knocked over or falling.

At first we were way in the lead, but cutting through yards alone and cutting through yards weighed down with a mattress are two different things. The high drifts by the sidewalks slowed us down to a terrifying crawl when we tried to get over them. Each time that we almost lost the mugs, we would find ourselves having to struggle over a drift, and then we would hear one of them shout as he saw us again.

"They're sticking too close," I yelled to Jack. Poor Jack's face was scarlet from doing most of the pulling and hoisting of the mattress. He was sweating.

"Suicide Hill," he gasped. "Step on it!"

Suicide Hill was dotted with sledders and tobogganers. It glistened in the late afternoon sunshine like a sheet of polished glass.

We'd have to risk it. It would be the only way to gain distance on the clumsy men without giving Jack a heart attack. Those mugs would have a hard time following us down that hill.

They were closing mighty fast, so we sprinted for it down Springman Drive to the top of the hill.

"Gangway!" Jack yelled. We threw the mattress over the summit and dived after it. The top coating of the hill was still wet from the morning thaw. It gave us plenty of good speed; I think we must have flown in places. My hand found the cloth handle on the side

and clutched it. I kept my other arm around Jack. I didn't dare look back for fear of the unexpected terrors that might lie ahead. Trees sprinkle the surface of Suicide Hill. But the mattress, fast as it was skimming and unsteerable as it was, held to the toboggan runway. I saw Annette as we flashed by. Her gossipy eyes were huge in her face. Jack couldn't resist bawling out, "The adoption agency is after us!"

The mattress slowed as the ground leveled, and then it dumped us, but we came up running with it. The hill had brought us closer to Sergeant McKenna's house.

"Keep to the roads. We'll race 'em now," Jack bawled. We skittered down the middle of one of the quiet streets of Peabody, keeping in the wheel ruts for good footing. I think Suicide Hill really stopped the crooks for a few minutes, because we were almost at Sergeant McKenna's driveway before we heard them shouting at us again.

We started yelling for him as soon as we set foot on his property, and he came quickly to the door. The mugs were right behind us. He didn't ask anything at first, just opened the door, and we tumbled into his house—mattress and all. Jack threw the mattress down on the living room floor and pulled out his pocket knife. He plunged it into the mattress.

"Watch out!" I yelled to Sergeant McKenna. The crooks ripped the front screen door off some of its hinges as they tore into the house. I had no doubts any more, once I saw their faces—them thinking this was our house and the sergeant was just an ordinary man. They were ready to rip us and the place apart. They turned to jump Sergeant McKenna, but next thing I knew Sergeant McKenna had his gun in his hand, ready as you please.

You always imagine cops saying "hold it right there," or "stop in the name of the law," but he just looked the three mugs square in their faces, and they calmed down.

"You have any reason to be chasing these kids?" he asked.

One of the thugs recovered himself and spoke up boldly, "You got any reason for pulling a gun on us, mister?"

"Two reasons—you just broke into my house, and I'm a police officer with a suspicious nature."

They backed down right away, then, even the bold one. There's something about Sergeant McKenna that does that to thugs. I used to wish he would do it to Scruggs Grady, too.

One of the guys, the big bald one who had kicked me out the day before, pointed down at the mattress that Jack had ripped apart.

"That kid stole my mattress. Lookit! Lookit what he's doing! You think I shouldn't get mad and rip off his front door to get my mattress back?"

"They're smugglers!" I said. "Honest, Sergeant McKenna!"

Two of the guys acted like they thought I was crazy, but the man who had driven the truck looked a little pale. None of them seemed worried that Jack was, by this time, plowing his hands through the guts of the mattress, looking for "the stuff."

"Smugglers?" McKenna exclaimed. I saw right away that he didn't believe us. He really had been kidding when he had told us to watch the mattress place. He slipped his gun back in its hiding place on the back of his belt.

"Right, smugglers, and I'll prove it any second now." Jack was still searching the mattress.

Then all of a sudden the mugs relaxed. They folded their arms and looked down at Jack, leering at him. I felt more than ever like they must be crooks—and not very smart crooks, either. But I had a sinking feeling that "the stuff," whatever it was, wasn't inside the mattresses.

Mrs. McKenna had come in from the kitchen when she heard all the fuss. "Beryl," the sergeant said to her, "call the Derwoods. Have them come up."

"Nothing," Jack lamented, looking up from the torn and ruined mattress.

"Go on, sonny, look some more. Maybe you missed a few places," the biggest mug jeered.

"Oh, be quiet!" I exclaimed.

"Penny!" Sergeant McKenna said sharply. "If you two took one of their mattresses and destroyed it over some game or notion, they have every right to be angry."

"It isn't a game or notion," I said. "They're smugglers all right, them and their two pals, Tom Thumb and Moses."

"What put them crazy names into your head?" the bald one asked. He sounded like he was jeering, too, but it looked to me like he really wanted to know.

"You figure it out," I said.

"That's enough, Penny. It looks to me like you two are in enough trouble."

I turned to Jack. He was still sitting on the floor, heartbroken. It was one of the few times I had ever seen my brother close to tears.

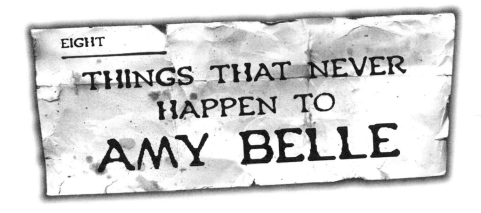

EIGHT

THINGS THAT NEVER HAPPEN TO AMY BELLE

Dad spanked us both for what we did. We saw it coming as soon as he walked into Sergeant McKenna's living room and heard the story. In his eyes, the worst thing was that we weren't sorry, and that always merits a spanking in our family.

As soon as he had walked into the McKennas' living room and had seen the wreck, he had announced that Jack and I would pay for the ruined mattress, of course. He paid the mugs for us, and we would pay him back with all the money we had and by working it off.

That had pleased the mugs. It looked to me like they were playing up to my father by acting like they respected authority. But Dad didn't see the dirty looks and smirks they'd been giving the sergeant when they didn't think anybody was looking. And he hadn't seen their faces before they'd found out Sergeant McKenna had a gun. They'd been ready to rip the house apart, then.

After Dad apologized to them, they started to pick up the ruined mattress to take it with them, but Jack set his foot on it.

"If I pay for it, I keep it," he said stoutly. "That's only fair."

"Jack!" Dad exclaimed.

Sergeant McKenna took an unexpected hand in things. "The boy's right," he said to the mugs. "If he and his sister pay for it, it's theirs. You couldn't possibly want it now, could you?" And his frank blue eyes looked right at them. So Sergeant McKenna did suspect them, I thought.

Dad looked more embarrassed and upset than ever, but he didn't make an argument of it. The three mattress-store mugs looked pretty agitated. They didn't know quite what to do. I could see as plain as day that they wanted that mattress. Sergeant McKenna made a polite suggestion by pulling open the front door. Not having much choice, they ambled out, but they sure hated to leave that ruined mattress behind.

Sergeant McKenna offered to keep the mattress for us, and Jack almost said no, but then the sergeant added, "It will pay for my screen door. Let me keep the mattress, and I'll call it square."

Dad overruled Jack and said that would be fine.

Dad took us home, and—like I said—he spanked us. Then he told us we had to go to bed right after supper for the next two weeks. And in the meanwhile, we had to come up with ways to work off the mattress bill.

Then he talked to us and reasoned with us, and that was the hardest thing, because it really looked to him like we had stolen the mattress and weren't sorry for it. And the more we tried to explain, the more upset he became.

"The least of my worries is that you made nuisances of yourselves by reading too many detective novels," he said, pacing back and forth. "But to think of you locking men in their own store, and treating their property in such a shameful way, and then excusing yourselves by calling them names—"

"But, Dad," Jack said. "I told you I heard them talking—"

"And to eavesdrop!" he exclaimed. "To sneak into their store like a crook and hide. What proof did you have that they were doing anything illegal? Don't you have any more respect for people than that—to make up all kinds of stories about them being crooks? You two have been living in a fantasy world."

I said nothing after that because I didn't want to talk back to him. It was clear what he thought of our story—and, really, we had ruined our own believability by all the crazy things we'd done, like taking the mattress and ripping it apart. But I knew we were right about those guys. I just couldn't think of the right way to present it to Dad.

At last he sent us to our rooms. Mom was upset, too, but after I was in bed, feeling lonely and wronged and miserable, she came in and sat by my bed, said my evening prayers with me, and kissed me good-night like I was Freddy. Then she sat a while longer, smoothing back my hair and not saying anything much, though there was plenty she might have said. At last she went to go look in on Jack. I thought she was a very kind woman, something like a good fairy that night, and every bit my mother.

The next morning Jack and I still felt in disgrace. The others kept very still at breakfast, and nobody said anything much. But when the six of us were going out the door to go to school, Mom gave both Jack and me an extra squeeze.

We let Jean and the little ones walk ahead of us so that we could talk privately.

"It's my fault you got paddled," Jack began.

"No it isn't. I was as much in on it as you."

"Hmf," he replied. Then he added, "Those guys are crooks."

"Yeah, but we've blown our cover for sure now."

Traffic was usually slow on our street, so we looked up as a car came by. It slowed to a stop.

"Hey, kids!" Sergeant McKenna said, rolling down his window. We all stopped to say hello, and he talked to all six of us for a little bit, then looked keenly at Jack and me.

"Hop in, you two," he said. "Front seat."

We ran around to the other side and climbed in. Jean and the younger ones looked disappointed.

"Next time we'll all go for a ride," he promised them. "Today I have to talk to my two deputies." It wasn't so bad when he called us his deputies.

"Things are looking up," Jack whispered to me.

"Well," he said as he turned the car around. "First I want to tell you two that there's a right way and a wrong way to do things. Even if I—a police officer— had had evidence that those men from the mattress place were smugglers, I couldn't have 'captured' one of their mattresses to prove it. If I had done what you did, I would have been suspended from the police force at the very least. Even an officer of the law can't do what he thinks is best without the proper authority backing him up. I would need a warrant to seize suspected goods from smugglers." He looked over at us. "I think you two kids are pretty smart and have your hearts in the right place, but you have to learn to do things the right way."

"Yes, sir," we both said soberly. I was glad he wasn't angry about his screen door getting half-torn off its hinges. And I was glad he didn't yell at us.

Suddenly he smiled. "I can go easy on you because I've been wanting a new screen door anyway. And besides, I think you two were basically right about those three. Something was going on. They wanted that mattress back. I took it in to the lab to be analyzed last night. Now, suppose you tell me about your little case and how you've gotten things worked out."

So Jack, feeling better, told him everything. It had been hard to explain it all to Dad, because he'd been so upset about it. But Sergeant McKenna wanted us to relax and let him know everything, so we told him everything we could think of, and then wracked our brains some more for details.

"Okay," he said when we'd finished. "What you heard in the closet seems sketchy. But it's obvious those men are up to something—whether or not it's smuggling."

"I wish we had some clue about Tom Thumb and Moses," Jack said.

"So do I." Sergeant McKenna had been driving around the block by our school, but at last he pulled in. "I just want you to realize that some of what you did was wrong. People can't take the law into their own hands."

We nodded and thanked him for the ride. As we crossed the playground together, Jack said, "I think we owe Dad an apology for what we did last night. And I think after we apologize, we should try to explain it to him again—maybe if *we* calm down, we can explain our story better."

"Good idea. I'll see you later."

We each went to our separate homerooms, and for a while we forgot our disgrace. I didn't see Jack at lunchtime recess—he was playing with the other boys. It looked to me like he felt better, and I was happy for that, too. I went off with some of my friends to help plan a party that I knew I wouldn't be allowed to attend because of my punishment.

After school there was no need to hurry home, now that our shoe-shining days were over. We walked around the long way, talking aimlessly about everything except the smugglers, still savoring the last moments of not being in trouble before we got home. This neighborhood was Scruggs's territory, but usually it was safe enough in the afternoons because the public high school got out so much later than our school.

We forgot that Scruggs played hooky all the time.

"Oh, no," Jack groaned as we saw a familiar figure saunter out from behind a car parked along the street. I turned quickly. Scruggs's two pals were coming up from behind.

"Worms," Jack moaned under his breath.

This time they stood all around us so that we couldn't get away.

"Well, if it isn't the shoe-shine kids," Scruggs said with a leer. "They look hungry to me." He dug his hand into his pocket, and I had a funny idea what he was going to pull out.

"Scruggs," Jack said urgently. "Can I make one plea to any sense of decency that might have accidentally lodged in your brain once upon a time?"

"Sure, Jacky. Plea all you want."

"Don't make my sister do it. I'll eat two—but don't make my sister eat one."

The insulting smile almost faded from Scruggs's face, even though his pals laughed at Jack. For myself, I wanted to yell, "We're partners! If there are any worms around here, I'll eat my share!" But I didn't say anything—not a peep. I had heard about Scruggs doing this, and I didn't want to eat a worm.

"As it turns out, I've got only one," he said, pulling one out of his pocket and dangling it in front of Jack. One of the mugs behind Jack suddenly shoved him. "Go on, hero, eat it, or we'll feed it to you."

Jack's hand darted out with lightning speed, so fast that for a minute I thought he was going to hit Scruggs. I think Scruggs thought so too, because he jerked his head back with a snap. But no, Jack had only snatched the worm with his right hand in a fierce gesture of defiance. He held Scruggs's eye with his own. I felt a surge of admiration for Jack—the eleven-year-old holding the fourteen-year-old in a glare of contempt like one I've never seen. And Scruggs—unbelievably—looked down, ashamed. I suddenly remembered something I had heard a long time ago—something about Scruggs having a sister. Long, long ago, when I was still on training wheels, before Scruggs had been a bully, there had been a little girl he had played with, drawing chalk pictures on the sidewalk.

Only for a moment Jack's hand faltered at his chest; then he brought it up and crammed it to his mouth. He looked Scruggs in the eye again, chewed and swallowed. The guys behind us were laughing really hard. They thought it was grotesque, but really funny, too. So far, I knew, the worm had only been an excuse for them to rough up little kids. Nobody had really eaten one before.

Scruggs looked a little sick. He mumbled something about it being a free world, and we could go, so we did—half-expecting them to tackle us from behind. But they didn't.

I started to cry. I put my arm around Jack and cried as we walked along. "Can't you spit the rest out?" I asked, sobbing. "Oh Jack, I'm sorry."

"Penny, you little mug," he said softly, putting his right arm around me. "Look up." I did, and there was the worm, uneaten, dangling in front of me, held in his left mitten.

I gasped and stopped crying. He grinned, triumphant for the first time since yesterday afternoon. "Don't you remember the sleight-of-hand book I read last summer while you were wasting your time on Amy Belle?" he asked. "That's why I had to snatch it so fast and make Scruggs think I might hit him—so I could drop it into my other hand before they looked down again."

I was amazed! All I remembered about the "sleight-of-hand" book was that he got in trouble with Mom for hurting Jean's feelings by using some of her hard cookies in his trick show. I never had appreciated Jack's taste in reading . . . at least not until lately.

"I thought for sure while I was faking my way through eating that worm they would guess it wasn't in my mouth." Jack dropped his hands and laughed weakly. "But it worked. We've done it again, partner!" He glanced behind him to make sure the bullies were gone, and then flung the worm out across the snow.

I thought again about how Scruggs had looked—ashamed, really. "Whatever happened to Scruggs's sister?" I asked suddenly.

"Huh? Oh, I don't know. He's a foster kid—maybe she went to another foster home." His mind dismissed the subject of Scruggs's sister. "Boy, just wait until I'm big enough to stand up to him, Penny."

"I hope it's soon."

We were walking across the entrance to a side street. I looked up in time to see a car skimming towards us.

"Watch out!" I exclaimed, pulling Jack back. "What's that guy doing?"

The car nearly ran over our toes as it cut straight across our path and skidded to a stop. It slammed into the curb. We jumped back to run away. Suddenly one of the cars along the street behind us came to life and made a turn in the street so that it also was blocking our way from behind. Without hesitation three men, the guys from the mattress store jumped out of the cars— two from the back car and one from the car in front of us.

"Penny, run!" Jack yelled and dived head first into the man coming toward us. But I was already caught, even as he said it.

"Help!" I started to yell, and then something wet was slapped hard across my face and held there. For a minute I thought I would smother. I felt a rush of sickness in the terribly sweet-smelling cloth, and then— I suppose—I fell asleep.

If you've ever had to wake up from surgery, you might have some idea of how I felt when I woke up— mighty sick. The room was swimming, and somehow from the minute my eyes opened, I could remember that I was in terrible danger. That made it worse.

"Now, now, if you try to get up, you'll make yourself sicker," somebody said to me, and I sank back onto a cold concrete floor and closed my eyes.

"That's my sister," I heard Jack say groggily. I forced my eyes open, and the first thing I saw was Jack, huddled on his side against a wall, shivering and looking ill. But he was all right—I mean, he was alive.

I experimented by lifting my head first. The room only rocked a little bit instead of pitching around. Then I brought my shoulders up, bracing myself on my elbow. Unexpectedly a hand slid behind my back and helped me up. "That chloroform is no fun," the voice said.

I looked up, even though the light from some kind of window hurt my eyes, and saw a woman next to me, helping me get oriented. For a moment she looked familiar, but I couldn't place her. With her help I managed to sit up and look around.

"Where are we?"

"An old factory," she said briskly. "Looks like it's been deserted for decades."

"Who are you?" I asked.

"A secret agent!" Jack guessed, eager and excited even in the middle of our problem. "You've been watching the mattress store, too!"

"Are you really?" I asked her. Maybe I had seen her hanging around.

"Well, a government agent, but not a very good one," she admitted humbly. "I got myself captured, just like you two, only I'm supposed to be trained not to let that happen." And she smiled a warm smile at me.

"Do they let girls be secret agents?" I asked. "Could I become one, do you think?"

She smiled again. "If we get out of here, I'll try to pull a few strings for you," she promised. She helped Jack huddle closer to us. This deserted building had no heat, and the cold just came penetrating through the bricks and concrete. I noticed that she had spread her coat over me. I should have given it back to her, but I was so cold, I decided that I wouldn't unless she asked for it.

"I've been up here since morning," she told us. "I went into their mattress store to plant some listening devices—"

"So those guys are smugglers, right?" Jack asked.

She hesitated only briefly. "Right. They are. I may as well be frank with you. You seem to know quite a bit. They chloroformed me in the store. I woke up here."

"It's a factory?" I asked.

She nodded. "There's a window over there in that dark corner. While there was still light, I could look out of it and see the rest of the place. It's an old factory or mill—very old." She pointed at the lighter window. "On that side there's only empty space."

Jack looked thoughtful. "Maybe this is that old mill we've passed going back and forth from the lake," he suggested to me. I knew right away the building he meant. It was about five miles out of Peabody. Most of it was bricked or boarded up.

Jack stood up and ventured into the dark corner that she said faced the rest of the building. Although pale, waning light was filtering from the window closer to us, that side of the room was already swathed in shadow. "There might be rats," she warned as he walked into the dimness.

"We're being held prisoner by three rats," he told her. He managed to catch hold of the ledge and lift himself up.

"Too dark on that side," he said, jumping down. "What time is it?"

She glanced at her watch. "Seven o'clock."

"What will they do to us?" I asked her.

She shrugged. "They haven't said a word to me since I've been in here."

Jack looked thoughtful. "There must be a railroad siding along here. There always is. Penny, maybe this is where the smugglers drop off their stuff—that place they talked about before."

Our companion looked a little alarmed. "My, but you're smart," she told him. "It took me a long time to figure that out."

"You mean they meet a train?" I asked Jack. "Wouldn't that mean that most of the people who work on the train would be in on this?"

"No," he said slowly. "Not if the train is scheduled to pick up freight cars here anyway—anything shipped out of Peabody to be headed north. This might be the pickup point of some of the freight cars. All the crooks have to do is load their stuff onto a half-empty car— or empty one out—and give it a fake invoice, and the regular freight train comes by and picks it up from the siding. Somebody further up the line claims the mattresses."

It had grown even darker in the last few minutes. I could barely see, but I could sense our new friend's amazement. It doesn't astonish me any more to see Jack's brilliance, but it is fun to watch him surprise other people.

"You should see him with worm tricks," I told her.

"Wouldn't I like to know what they've got hidden in those mattresses!" he exclaimed.

"Well, for me, I'd like to know why they kidnapcd us," I said, "and what they plan to do to us."

"It must have been terrifying when they trapped you between their cars," she said consolingly. I nodded and shivered. "You must know something that worries them," she told me. Something nagged at the back of my mind when she said that—something about knowing something.

"Hardly. We don't even know what they're hiding in those mattresses. We couldn't find anything," Jack told her. "But we knew they really wanted their mattress back."

"Really? They knew that you took one from them?"

"Oh, yeah. We captured it in broad daylight and ran to the nearest policeman with it, but we couldn't find anything. At first he thought we were crazy, but then those mugs gave themselves away by the way they acted," he told her. "They pulled his screen door almost all the way off its hinges."

"Hmmm. But then Sergeant McKenna just let them go?"

"Yeah," Jack sighed.

She laughed a little. "And you carted your mattress home with you?" she asked.

"Well, you see—" Jack began, ready to tell her how Dad had made us pay for it and everything. But suddenly everything came together in my mind.

"No!" I shouted. The cry echoed in the sudden stillness, and I found I had grabbed Jack's arm in the darkness. "Don't, Jack. Don't say it."

"Penny, what's wrong with you?"

It was too dark now to see her face, but I turned to where I knew she was. "How did you know, if you've been locked in here all day without talking to anybody, that they cut us off in their cars?" I asked her. "And how do you know that his name is Sergeant McKenna?"

Jack was absolutely still, numbed. Even she was quiet for a long moment. "You still want that mattress," I said at last. "You lost track of it last night when all those mugs had to walk back to the mattress store."

And then I heard her suck in her breath, angry at being so outwitted.

"Tom Thumb," I called her.

Jack moved closer to me in the darkness and took hold of my hand.

"Is that who you are?" he asked her.

Her voice changed its tone. "If you two brats want to live until tomorrow, you'd better tell me where it is."

Then suddenly I knew her. She was the tour guide from the button place . . . the lady who had scared me. I wondered if she recognized me as the seventh-grader who had wandered off.

Jack spoke up. "We're not afraid to die," he said clearly, but his voice was high.

Suddenly she stood up and switched a small flashlight on. I expected any moment for her to hit one of us, but after a long, steady moment when she must have been looking at us, she backed away toward the door.

"Open!" she called in a voice so full of anger and authority that no doubt was left in my mind about what she would do to us. "You two better be ready to cooperate by the time I come back," she said. The door opened, and she was gone, but it closed with a heartbreaking thud, and even across the room we could hear the noise of a chain being drawn and a padlock snapping into place. Two pairs of footsteps clumped away.

Next to me, Jack shuddered. "And to think we almost told her everything! Come on, get up," he told me. "This place is falling apart. Let's look around."

We groped along the walls in the darkness. The brick and mortar were old, and there were huge gaping cracks here and there, but nothing wide enough to squeeze through, and if we had squeezed through, there wouldn't have been anyplace to go. We were up high in the building, probably in what had once been offices. But the largest windows had been bricked up, and the two smaller ones looked out on nothing but space, although from the eastern one we could see shadowy roofing of other parts of the mill below us and to the side. As we searched, we kept tripping over debris on the floor. It was littered with bits of brick and other litter.

"It's no good," he said at last. "We can't get out from up here."

"Time for a little planning," I suggested. "Some of that sleight-of-hand you talked about."

"What?"

"She and her goons are going to come back soon."

"Yeah?"

"Well, maybe we can fool them. Take off your coat."

"What? And get pneumonia?"

"Hurry up!"

He took off his coat, and I took off mine. Then I crawled over and found the coat that she had left behind. "Let's make scarecrows, quick," I told him. "They've only got a flashlight to see us by. We can fool them long enough for us to get away."

We stuffed our coats with bricks, dirt, rags, and everything else we could find. We huddled them against the far wall and then piled other rubble against the wall. When we draped her coat over the rubble and patted it down in places, it looked like Jack's trousers—anyway it looked enough like them to fool people watching with a flashlight. We plumped up my tam and his cap for the heads.

We had the dummies in the lightest part of the room, under the western window, and we hoped that they would catch the eyes of the crooks first thing after the door was open.

Finally we hid alongside the door, which opened outward. We could already hear footsteps coming up a long stairway, and I realized that almost an hour must have passed since Lady Tom Thumb had left us. I felt Jack relax a moment, and I knew he was praying while they were coming up for us.

Then we heard the padlock being unlocked, and the door slowly swung away from us. We flattened against the wall, not even breathing. The pale flashlight beam cut into the room, checked one corner, the far wall, and then rested on the two dummies lying huddled under the western window.

"Let's get them on their feet. We'll take them to the loading dock where we've got Moses," Tom Thumb growled, and she and two of the mugs forged boldly into the room.

I was closest to the door, and as soon as they walked past me, I slipped behind them really gently, not making a sound. Then Jack whisked out, and they heard him. We slammed the door shut. I held it with my knee and foot, and Jack had all his weight against it while I fumbled with the lock and at last clicked it shut. I gave it a yank to make sure it was secure; then we ran to the landing and the steps.

"There's one more of them somewhere," Jack gasped. "We only trapped her and two of the men."

"And Moses, he might be lurking around," I added. "They said he's on the loading dock."

"Let's hope he stays there," Jack said. "From what I could tell, we're facing the highway, and I think the loading dock is on the other side of the building."

We found a black abyss, unlighted by windows, which we took to be the steps. I clutched the railing and inched one toe down, felt a solid step, repeated the process with the other foot, felt a second step. Above us, we could hear the men throwing their weight against the door of their prison.

"They'll break the door down soon," I said. "We've got to run."

Our eyes couldn't pierce the darkness at all on the steps. It was like being blind, but they felt solid at least, so we hurried, ran down seven steps, and tripped on a landing, smashing into a wall. We groped around for the next flight of steps, but now we knew the secret— ten steps to a flight. We counted ten more as we ran and expertly took a complete turn to the left, where we found the next flight, ten steps more, a turn to the left, and so on.

At last we took a turn to the left and smashed into a brick wall. It knocked us back.

"Ground floor!" Jack announced dizzily. We began to feel around for a hallway or something. Above us, like thunder from miles away, the door was broken down.

"They're really going to be mad now," he said.

We hurried. My fingers felt a change in the rough concrete—a seam where it ended and linoleum began. "Found a hallway!" I hissed. We held hands and ran up the hallway, keeping our feet high because of debris.

Even so I twisted my ankle several times, and often I caught Jack when he stumbled. But we managed.

They had the flashlight and could move much faster in the dark building. Our only hope, we knew, was to get outside where the light from the snow would help us. But we had no coats.

We saw a window ahead where the boards must have been torn away by vandals. Jack quickly hoisted me up the sill, and I jumped out without even looking. The drop outside was higher than the climb inside by about three feet, so I got the wind knocked out of me. Then he dropped down beside me, and we were in the monstrously huge courtyard of the mill.

"The tracks," Jack panted. "A train might come— we could catch onto it."

I nodded. Just then, we saw the tracks, running smoothly alongside the length of the mill, but we stopped short. Tom Thumb was out there with her two mugs, scanning the courtyard. We dropped into the shadows that clung along the many corners of the building.

"Scratch that idea," he said.

She turned and scanned the courtyard. Time after time her eyes swept past us.

"Don't move, Jack," I whispered.

"Why? Is there a spider on me?"

"No, you mug. She's looking over this way." I couldn't figure out how he could make jokes at a time like this.

Her eyes scanned right past us. But I was worried. We'd given her the big tip-off: our brains. That's one thing Amy Belle never does. She never lets anybody know how much she's been studying to be a detective. You never see her mention it in one of her books. Jack and

I—fools through and through—had been showing off that we'd been reading books on sleuthing for the past four years.

At last they walked away, but we were no better off. Somewhere there was another mug, and they would surely be watching the tracks. We sat there in the freezing darkness, panting and shivering. "Well, we found out who Tom Thumb is," I said. But at least we didn't have to worry about that Moses mug. Jack had been right— the loading dock was on the other side of the building.

Jack must have been thinking the same thing. "I hope that Moses stays where he is," he said. "You figure he's an agent?"

"Shhhhh. I hear something." We strained to listen. Jack slipped his hand over mine.

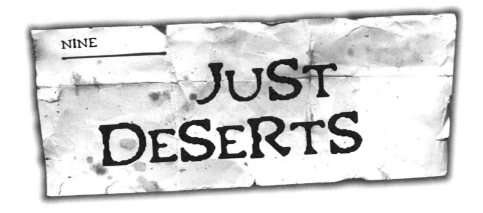

NINE

JUST DESERTS

From far away we heard a truck coming. I figured that was where the third guy had been, picking up a load of mattresses for delivery. Soon, the big truck rolled into the courtyard. We shrank back from the headlight beams, which narrowly missed us. The driver cut the engine and climbed out. Our hearts sank as we saw him pocket the keys.

The two others and Tom Thumb came up to him while Jack and I huddled in the shadows to be as small as possible. Tom Thumb would have done better with a code name like Captain Hook. She was blaming everybody but herself for our escape and giving orders for them to search for us. But then she glanced at her watch, and she said something about the freight car's not being loaded yet and get a move on. Hastily, the driver ran back to the truck and started it. He swung it around and backed it up to the siding. Only in swinging it around did he rake us with the headlight beams, but his head was craning the other way, watching the rear, where he was going. I was very thankful he was a careful driver.

He backed it along the siding to a boxcar that was waiting with its doors open. He didn't quite have the truck in position for loading when Tom Thumb gave a yell. She had spotted a passenger train coming along the opposite tracks.

At her words my heart leaped and then sank. There would be no way we could escape to it. We'd have to run across the siding and one set of tracks.

Tom Thumb directed two of the men to the mill entrances that were facing the tracks. So, she supposed us to be inside, I realized. She was thinking we might burst out from the doors and make a run for it.

"Come with me!" she shouted to the man backing up the truck. He hurriedly slipped it into neutral and put the brake on. Jack and I looked at each other.

Up ahead the train was coming slowly around a bend that had a sharp curve to it. It made her nervous. She and the driver weren't far from the truck, but they did have their backs to it as they watched the train. And the other men, I was pretty sure, couldn't even see the truck from where they were stationed. It wasn't nearly as big as an eighteen wheeler, and we only had to get it as far as civilization to get help.

"Do you understand a clutch?" I whispered to Jack.

"I've used one on a dirt bike before," he whispered back. "And I've watched Dad."

"You work the pedals."

We crept out, walking easily and light, not running. To run would have betrayed us. We were on the south side of the building, and the snow was shallow where it hadn't drifted. As the train came nearer, the racket got louder and louder until we didn't have to be as careful about our footsteps. The truck looked safer and safer

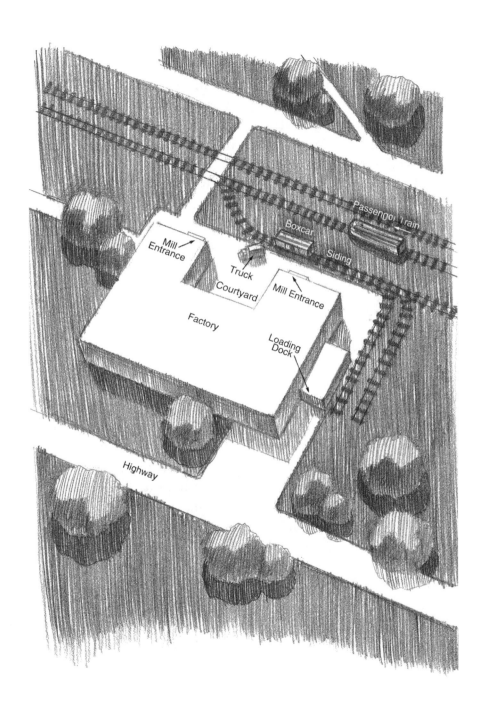

as we crept toward it—like a mirage or something unreal. Its driver side door was open.

Tom Thumb was pointing down to a lone tree by the mill, wondering if it was us hiding in its shadow. She was practically shouting over the roar of the train. We hurried. Now the train was thundering down on us, now past us. We leaped into the truck—Jack first. I banged the door closed. Jack pushed on the clutch, and I kicked his foot off the gas while I went into first gear. With a wrench and a bang we started forward. Then I let him hit the gas as much as he wanted to while we ran parallel to the tracks with that bigger-than-life train coming along our right.

"Left! Left! Left!" Jack screamed in my ear. Something pinged off the roof of the truck.

"Shift! Shift!" I bawled. "They're chasing us!"

He shifted us up one more—I think from second gear right into fifth, but I'm not sure.

"Gas! Gas!" I yelled. He was half off the seat, pushing down on the pedals while I worked the big wheel. We almost did careen into the side of the train, but I swerved just in time and saw the road up ahead. I thought I heard gunshots but couldn't tell. My fingers found a knob and pulled it, and the wipers came on. They found another knob and the lights came on.

"Look in the mirror! Are they coming?" I yelled.

"How can I look in the mirror when I'm half on the floor!" he yelled. "Left, left, we're almost in the ditch!"

"Now we're in the middle of the road!" I veered back to the right. He shut his eyes. "Brake! Gimme brakes! I've got to turn!" I yelled. The sign up ahead pointed to the right. It said "Peabody, 5 miles."

"Five miles of this!" he moaned. He hit the brake too softly, and we swerved around a telephone pole on the corner before we made the turn.

The next two miles were smooth running on a flat, clear road, and I felt like we were doing about eighty. We discovered that, even with the worst danger over, we couldn't drive right. We either almost ran into the ditch or had to ride down the middle of the road. At last my nerve failed me. I wanted a safe way home. I made Jack slow us down to a crawl—about five miles an hour—and then turned the truck into a small grocery store. Even then he hit the brake too softly, and our tires slammed into the curb. We climbed out and ran to a phone booth to call for help.

"Who first?" Jack asked as he dialed the pay phone.

"Mom and Dad."

"Then who?" Jack spread out all his change on the ledge by the phone.

"The police. And tell them to let Sergeant McKenna know."

"Then who?"

"Bill Tucker from church. He likes trucks. Oh, and call Mr. Scott."

"I'll call the deacon board, too. That way we'll get into the bulletin."

We called everybody we could think of, so if the smugglers had come after us, we would have a small army assembled.

Jack had just finished telling Mr. Scott about it when Dad pulled up. A patrol car came in right behind him. Then Sergeant McKenna pulled in, followed by the Tuckers. Four more police cars went screaming past, headed for the mill, I supposed.

Dad had us in his arms hugging us. It was only then that I realized it was almost ten o'clock and I was both hungry and numb from cold.

* * * * * *

The kitchen was crowded with three reporters, eight policemen, the deacon board, Mom and Dad, and a sixteen-inch pizza—the box, anyway. Jack and I had finished the pizza. We were working on our second pot of hot cocoa.

Sergeant McKenna stumped in. "Been knocking a while," he said. "Finally gave up and came right in."

Mom apologized, but Dad laughed and said, "Guess it is a little noisy." Then he smiled again, slapped our shoulders, and pinched our ears.

"This is better than in Amy Belle," I whispered to Jack. "What else can we tell them?" Jack had done most of the talking, but I'd surprised even him when I told everyone about meeting Tom Thumb months ago at the button factory.

"Let's get the sergeant to deputize us," Jack whispered back. "And later, when we get him alone, let's ask him about Moses. The police must not have found anybody out there at the loading dock."

"Sergeant McKenna!" we called.

He smiled. "Looks like you kids are recovering from your scare just fine. How'd you like an update?"

The reporters had been looking around, observing details, I suppose, but their heads jerked up at this.

"We got the three men from the mattress store, but Lady Tom Thumb slipped through our dragnet," he said. "Soon as she saw that truck making tracks, she must have figured it was every man for himself—ladies, too.

She caught hold of that passenger train and escaped. The other three weren't so smart."

"Do you know who she is, Sergeant?" I asked.

"Well, we have an idea from the description you gave us. I'll take you in to headquarters tomorrow to show you some pictures of her. Sounds to me like she's one Susan Elizabeth Walters, a brilliant mathematician and computer scientist who defected a couple years ago to the Eastern Block."

"Computer scientist." Jack's eyes narrowed. He looked thoughtful.

"Was she masterminding the mattress operation?" I asked.

"Oh, no. They were all part of a smuggling ring, just like you said. They were getting high technology out of the United States into other countries illegally. She's probably what you might call a shop manager— she oversees several operations bases."

"Well then," Jack said. "That might answer one question about where they were hiding the stuff in the mattresses."

Sergeant McKenna beamed. "I just got my report from the lab, but I'll let you take a guess before I tell you."

"The buttons sewn onto the tops of the mattresses," he guessed. "That's why Tom Thumb was working in that factory. She was making her own special buttons."

All the reporters and most of the deacons looked at Sergeant McKenna. He nodded once. "You've got it. They were sending microchips out. The chips were sealed in plastic, coated over and over again to look like buttons, and then attached to the mattresses."

"Microchips?" one of the reporters exclaimed. "What was on them? Government secrets? Plans of some sort?"

Sergeant McKenna opened his hands. "That's all I can say, really. I'm just a local cop who'll be called to testify. You boys will be dealing with government agents from now on," he told the reporters. "I heard rumors that the microchips were processors stolen from some top American corporations, but I couldn't say anything official."

The reporters left, and—after they saw that the cocoa was gone—the other policemen did too, with most of the deacons. Now was my chance to perfect my grown-up voice.

"We have two things to talk to you about," I said. Sergeant McKenna put down his cup of hot chocolate and gave us his full attention. "First, what about that Moses guy? Did anybody catch him or see him?" I asked.

"No," he told me. "Of course we'll search the place several more times. But Moses may have flown the coop with Tom Thumb. I guess they're both long gone. What's the second thing on your agenda?" he wanted to know.

"Will you deputize us?" Jack begged.

He put his huge hands on his waist and squared his shoulders. "What?" he pretended to roar. "So you can heist mattresses and break every traffic law in Wisconsin again?"

"No, so we can be one up on Amy Belle," I said.

"Do we get badges?" Jack asked.

"No, you don't get badges! Well—" He caught himself. "Let me think about it." He glanced at Dad, and Dad nodded slightly, as though giving in. But the sergeant only shrugged a little and changed the subject.

"We'll beef up a patrol on this street until we know where Lady Tom Thumb and Moses have gotten to," he said. "I guess once is enough for being kidnaped."

"I'll say!" Jack exclaimed. "Say, did anybody take care of Harry while I was gone?"

"Yes, yes," Mom assured him. "I looked after your hamster today. He ran on his wheel a little tonight."

Jack looked relieved. Ever since Jack had read an article about hamsters hibernating and dying after two years, he had been working on the theory that if he could prevent Harry from hibernating then Harry would live longer. Harry's two-year life span was almost over, so he was right at the "crucial period," as Jack called it. We had finally taught Sherwood, our cat, to leave Harry alone. Now it was just a matter of keeping Harry awake and measuring his time upon this earth.

"Well," Dad said after everybody else had left. "I suppose I'll have to learn to live with crime busters until this phase wears off."

Mom smiled. "I once lived with one for a while."

"Was that when you were little, Mom?" I asked. "With Aunt Whatshername?"

"Aunt Irene, Penny, not Aunt Whatshername," she corrected gently.

Dad laughed. "I only met her once—what a lady!" That's what he said every time he talked about Aunt Irene—"What a lady!" Whenever Mom had a family reunion and all her brothers and sisters who lived close enough came to visit (eight of them lived close enough), we heard all kinds of stories about my Aunt Irene. I thought from the way everybody talked about how tough and crusty she was that they were exaggerating. But my Uncle Bill from California, who I only met once, wagged his head at me when I said that to him, and told me, "No, Penny, you haven't heard the half of it. Your mother doesn't rightly remember half the things about your Aunt Irene." His eyes twinkled at me, but he told me I was too young to understand.

"Why was Aunt Irene a crime buster, Mom?" I asked.

"Dear me, it's one o'clock in the morning, Penny. I can't tell you that long story now," she said. "And I don't know it that well myself. Next time your Uncle Bill visits, you'll have to ask him to tell you all about her."

Mom's mother had died right after Mom—the twelfth in the family—had been born. Aunt Irene had raised Mom for a little while before sending her away to relatives in Wisconsin. Bit by bit she had sent the other brothers and sisters out the same way to work for the same relatives and earn their educations. Now most of them lived around Peabody, but Aunt Irene still kept the same old house somewhere in Pennsylvania.

Dad said she was something of a recluse, but I didn't know what that meant. Anyway, we had our Aunt Miriam close by. She wasn't married, and she always came over for birthdays and made our favorite cakes for us.

I never even thought about not being really related to Aunt Miriam or to any of Mom's brothers and sisters. They never acted any differently toward us, and I'm sure—with all the nieces and nephews in a family of twelve brothers and sisters—that some of them even forgot which ones were the stepchildren.

Dad yawned. "Yeah, even if I have to learn to live with crime busters, I still want my sleep. To bed, you two. We can talk more in the morning."

"Dad, now that you know the whole story better, are you still upset with us?" I asked. "We really are sorry for the wrong things we did."

"I know, and no, I'm not upset with you. I see now that you were right about some things. But I still want you to pay for the mattress by working it off."

"Because it was wrong to take it the way we took it?" I asked.

"No, because I need help around the house." He laughed at his own joke and then added soberly, "Yes, because I want you to understand that you should never take anything—even for a good purpose—if you have no right to it."

He was walking with me to the bottom of the stairs when Mom put in, "Oh, I have some work for them. The Ladies' Auxiliary Missionary Fellowship is having their luncheon meeting here next week. Penny and Jack can help serve. That ought to be worth something off their debt."

Jack sighed. "I'd rather spend Saturday at Big Sand Lake."

I couldn't believe my ears. Not even the Ladies' Auxiliary Missionary Fellowship Luncheon could be as dull as another weekend at Big Sand Lake. Things just weren't the same up there without the fifty-ton, mile-long, giant killer octopus.

"Now, Jack," she reproved him. "We must do our part, especially with Mrs. Tucker still recuperating. You two can do well under my supervision."

"Remind me to have a business luncheon that day," Dad said under his breath. Then he added so that she could hear him, "We'd better move it up a week or two.

I'm sure things won't be settled enough by next Saturday for you to be hostessing a church luncheon."

"Oh, that's right. I had better postpone it at least another week."

We kissed them good night and went upstairs, just in time to hear everybody else make a mad scramble into their beds from the top of the stairs.

"Oh boy," Jack mumbled. "The Derwood Junior Spy Academy." He looked into the girls' room and said goodnight. I peeked in on Freddy before I went into my room.

The first thing I noticed when I switched on the light was my row of Amy Belle books on the little bookcase that Jean and I shared. Jean rolled over and pretended to be just waking up. She watched me as I experimentally tossed an Amy Belle book into the trash can.

"Hey!" She sat bolt upright. "Don't do that, Penny! Those are good books!"

"Sorry." I fished it out of the can. "I just wanted to see how it felt." I put it back on the shelf. I wasn't ready to give up Amy Belle just yet.

Jean watched me as I got ready for bed, and I had the idea that she had grown from being my little sister to being my newest admirer. With the others, she had been sent up to bed after the first hullabaloo over our return was ended, and she was hoping to pick up the rest of the story from me now. I sat on the edge of her bed and told her about it.

"Boy, we're glad you and Jack are O.K.," she said at last, when I'd finished and the clock read 2:00 A.M. "But you and Jack have more to be thankful for."

"What's that?"

"Well, you're so close to each other. I'm not close with anybody."

I kind of winced when she said it. It was true. Jean was too old to really have much fun with the younger three, and usually she was too young for Jack and me. Besides, Jack was impatient with her a lot of times— surprisingly impatient, for Jack.

"Well, we can do some things together," I consoled her. "Jack and I have to help Mom get ready for that luncheon thing next week. Maybe you can help with that."

She nodded, somewhat satisfied, but only halfway consoled. I admitted to myself that sometimes I was hard on Jean. Jack and I had been raised together, but she had come into the family as an only child and had gone from being the youngest to being the middle. Just the same she would have a hard time enjoying an adventure with Jack.

Jean was the sort of person who had perfect attendance certificates all the way back through nursery school. She had never gotten lower than an eighty on a test. The very idea of risking her neck to capture a mattress or of hiding in a closet for two hours would make her burst out crying. She just wasn't an adventurer.

"You see," I told her. "It's easy for me to be close with Jack because of what he does for me." And then I told her how he had asked Scruggs to let me off earlier that afternoon, and how he had dived at one of the thugs so that I could try to escape. "But," I added, "I try to do the same for him. Like shining shoes—which I hate—and hiding behind trash cans for an afternoon, and letting myself get paddled when I could try to put all the blame on him. That's part of being friends."

She got a little wide-eyed at that. I could see she was definitely going to have to rethink this buddy-buddy business. One thing Jean hated to take was risks.

"Well, it really does sound like you two had a lot of fun," she said at last. "But maybe it was awful while it was happening."

"Kind of," I agreed. Before I thought twice, I bent down and kissed her. I really was glad to be back. "Good night."

"Good night."

PART TWO

TEN

THE LADIES' AUXILIARY MISSIONARY FELLOWSHIP ANNUAL LUNCHEON

Sergeant McKenna reported that he'd searched the mill again and didn't find anybody. He told us maybe we'd misunderstood a code word or something. I had the feeling that he wasn't very worried, and I decided that he might just be right. "Moses" may very well have been their code name for money or tools or something.

Jack and I were duly deputized by Sergeant McKenna, and the reporters liked the idea so much that they took our pictures while he swore us in. But it didn't take more than a few days for us to realize that being deputized doesn't mean that much when crime is slow. It didn't give us any special privileges to investigate anywhere, and it didn't make anybody on the police force especially interested in calling on us for the tough cases.

I could understand that. In Peabody there are very few cases at all, and I'm sure they have to be divided up carefully according to seniority, and then prolonged as much as possible to make them last. But we were still disappointed.

Like I said, we got our pictures in the paper every day for a week, and the town council put a thousand dollars in trust for us for college. "In trust" means that nobody trusts you to spend it yet. We had to wait for college.

Some rich guys who had been born in Peabody and made a fortune in shipping on the Great Lakes put another five thousand dollars in trust for us. The thought of having all that money and not being able to spend it nearly killed us.

Other than that, nothing happened. We were still broke from paying Dad back; our shoe-shine kit had been destroyed; and to top it off, we got a spring snow. It bothered Jack even more than it bothered me.

"I'm so tired of snow!" he exclaimed one day after school. "I'm tired of dingy white all over everything! Dingy, grayish white!" He stalked away from me like it was my fault.

"Where are you going?" I called.

"To find something to do."

And then he was gone. I walked home alone, figuring that if I got kidnaped again it would serve him right. But nobody kidnaped me, and I got home safely. Jack came back a little later, all smiles.

"What's got into you?" I asked.

"I got a job," he said, pleased with himself.

"Why?"

"Because money is green. I can look at it instead of this snow. Besides, it'll pay us off quicker."

"What's the job?"

"Dog walking. Every weekday from three to three thirty with an option for dog-sitting until five." He bowed and went to ask Mom.

"It's okay, as long as you can help on Saturday with the luncheon," she said anxiously. The luncheon had already been postponed twice—once when Mrs. Tucker broke her leg and once because of all the excitement and fuss over the smugglers.

"I'll be free," he promised her.

"Have you got any dogs yet?" I asked.

"Four: two poodles named Bowser and Wowser, a schnauzer named Noodle, and an Irish wolfhound named Bruno."

"Sounds great," I said, and Mom nodded. But we were wrong. It wasn't great. It turned out to be terrible. The poodles, Bowser and Wowser, hated the schnauzer, Noodle. All three of them hated Bruno, who loved everybody.

For one thing, our cat, Sherwood Derwood, didn't want to make room for the dogs. Sherwood was mostly a house cat, and she'd never been forced to share before. She'd also never been chased by a dog before, and she didn't know what dogs were. The very first day, she hissed and spat at them and flew right at Bowser and Wowser while the schnauzer, Noodle, hid. Bruno chased her just for the fun of it, and she got really mad. She hid under the house for two hours.

Our second problem was that from the very first day Bruno was playing with everything in our yard—going wild in the snow. So on Friday, when Bruno galloped through the snowy yard and got his teeth into the gingham curtains hanging on the line, Mom came rushing out of the house faster than Sherwood had rushed into it at sight of the dog.

"Bad dog!" she exclaimed, and hit him across his shoulder with her hand. He kept tugging on the curtains. Then she clunked him across the head with one of her Dr. Finnegan's Comfortable Shoes.

That got his attention.

He barked and jumped up to lick her face. Apparently he thought she was playing with him.

But when two-hundred-plus pounds of Irish wolf-hound hit her—and her with one foot bare and standing on snow—she hit the ground . . . hard.

I saw it from the dining room and came rushing out the sliding back door.

"Mom! Mom!" I yelled. Jack was running to her from the other side of the lawn. Bruno thought it was a game of dog tag, and he went barking and jumping all over the yard, flinging snow off his paws.

"Are you all right?" I asked, trying to help her up.

"Don't, Penny," she said suddenly. "I think I broke something."

"Quick, Jack! Call the ambulance!" I screamed.

"Right!" He raced for the house. "I'll get you a good rate!"

"Hurry up, Jack!" I yelled. "What should I do, Mom?" I asked.

"Go turn the roast before you do anything. If I burn one more roast, I'll never forgive myself."

"Right!" I started off, then turned around. "Isn't there something else? Like hot tea? Blankets?"

"Yes, yes, Penny, but first the roast!"

I came out again as quickly as I could, tugging all the blankets that I could find.

Jack finally reappeared. No doubt he had been calling around to the different ambulance companies, trying to get all the rates.

"How's the roast?" she asked as I spread blankets over her and tucked them in to keep her dry. "Make sure you use a half cup of milk in the potatoes. Your father doesn't like them lumpy, you know."

"I like the lumps," Jack said mournfully.

"But Daddy's the head of the house, honey. You can have lumpy potatoes on Tuesday when he's at the deacons' dinner."

Just then we heard sirens, and Jean wandered out into the yard. "Mom, are you sick?" she asked.

"Mom fell," I said. "We think something's broken."

I carefully wrapped her bare foot up in one of the spare blankets. "Ah," she said with a contented sigh. "My, I haven't been able to lie down all day!"

"What happened to your shoe?" Jean asked, puzzled.

"Jack," I said, jumping up. "Those aren't ambulances coming—those are fire engines!"

"I know. See, whenever the fire engines go to a call, they bring an ambulance with them, and the fire company only charges a hundred dollars for the total call, but the ambulance companies alone charge—"

"Jack!" Mom's face went gray. "You didn't tell them the house was on fire, did you?"

"Of course not! But the dispatcher said that nobody was doing anything down there anyway, so they'd come."

"Oh," she said. "I was so afraid they would be angry or arrest you or—"

"Is it that easy to get arrested, Mom?" Jean asked. She looked interested.

"Don't you dare try anything, young lady—"

Just then four firemen and two men in white came stomping through the house. The firemen were all dressed up in black and red, with big axes.

"Oh boy, there she is!" one of them exclaimed. The two paramedics scowled at him. Nothing this exciting ever happens in Peabody, but they like to act like it does. The two medics knelt down by Mom and strapped a blood pressure cuff around her arm. One of them took out a little white card and made notes while the four firemen went sniffing around the yard and in the house, just to make sure nothing was really on fire.

The medics told Mom she had probably hurt her back, but it didn't look too bad—she'd be better in a few weeks.

"A few weeks!" she squawked. "Why, the Ladies' Auxiliary Missionary Fellowship Annual Luncheon Meeting is tomorrow!"

"Oh, you'll have to miss that, ma'am," one of the medics said.

"Miss it? I'm giving it! They're coming to my house tomorrow at eleven!"

The four firemen came back, wanting to help with the stretcher and backboard. All six of them lifted Mom, backboard and all, onto the stretcher and tied her in.

Then they wheeled her through the house and into the ambulance. Of course all the neighbors were out there, staring. The firemen sucked in their stomachs and looked especially serious.

"Penny, go turn that roast!" Mom exclaimed as they lifted the stretcher and loaded her up. "And tell Daddy not to worry. And tell Jean and Jack and Freddy and Renee and Marie not to worry either."

"Shouldn't I go with you, Mom?" I asked, coming to the back of the ambulance. "I mean, will you be all right?"

"Oh, I'm all right, honey. Tell Daddy to come tonight. Don't worry about me, sweetie—" A new thought struck her. "Worry about the Luncheon Meeting! Oooh!" She wailed.

As the medics and all the firemen climbed in and closed the door, I could hear her asking them if they thought she would have time to order a couple of pies and a cold-cut platter before tomorrow.

Mom called that night, and the first thing she asked about was how the roast had turned out, so I knew she was okay. Dad was already with her, but kids weren't allowed to visit at night.

"I'll be home in a few days," she said cheerfully. "It's just the Ladies' Auxiliary Missionary Fellowship Annual Luncheon Meeting that I'm thinking about."

"Oh, Mom," I said. "Dad can order the cold cuts, and we can come up with some desserts, right?"

"Well, all right. Have your brothers and sisters help you. And make them mind their manners tomorrow."

"I will."

"Some of those dear ladies are elderly, so don't shock them."

"I'll do my best."

"You'd better not let Jean cook anything. That ought to save everybody from the major shocks."

The next day Dad offered to take the three little kids out for lunch and to the park while Jack and Jean and I got ready for the luncheon.

"Miss Banks will give a speech, and Miss Crumble will preside, and there you are, sweetheart," he said, kissing me on the forehead after delivering a stack of wrapped cold cuts to the kitchen. "Now we'll get out of your hair and let you handle it. All right, deputies of Derwood, Incorporated?"

We saluted. "Aye, aye, Dad."

He smiled and hustled the three little ones out. The door closed behind them with a bang. I felt it down to my stomach as I realized that Mom and Dad were gone and we had to get ready for the Ladies' Auxiliary Missionary Fellowship Annual Luncheon—alone. In the sudden silence Jack spoke first.

"Are we charging for this thing?"

"No," I told him, "and don't even suggest it!"

"What a grouch!" He stomped to the kitchen. "I almost ate a worm for you, you know."

Jean was already busy cutting flour and shortening together—four pounds of flour and everything left in the can of shortening.

"Uh, Jean?" I began.

"Huh?" she asked, only half-listening.

"I don't think those little old ladies could possibly eat this much. They aren't lumberjacks."

She shrugged. "We can freeze it."

Jack picked up a piece of the dough. He held it out at arm's length and let it drop to the counter. It landed with a lifeless plop. "We could fix the ceiling with it."

She glared at him, hurt.

"Be nice, Jack," I said, wheedling.

"I was just kidding, Jean," he said. "I'll help you make a cherry pie, how's that?"

"Can you slice the rolls and bread too?" I asked. "I'll set the table and arrange the cold cuts."

"Roger!" He went to work with Jean on the pie. I didn't think much could go wrong with that, as long as Jack was in charge. He can read a recipe. I finished setting the table while the two of them moved on to slicing the bread.

Things went smoothly. I opened the refrigerator and took out the cold cuts.

I arranged the platter and put it back in the refrigerator. Jack was making apple turnovers by then with the filling Mom had made the day before. He was pretty good at the shells. Jean took the cherry pie out of the oven.

"I know," she said eagerly. "Let's cut it up and put the little pieces on individual plates!"

"Why should we do that?" I asked.

"So we can all have a piece, and nobody will notice," she replied.

Jack shook hands with her. "You're pretty smart," he said. He looked at me.

"Okay," I said.

So we did it, and it was a good thing we did. Jack took one bite of his, ran to the sink, and spit it out.

"Oh!" Jean exclaimed. "Jack—"

"What is it?" I asked.

He was still coughing. "Medicine!" he cried. "It tastes like medicine! No sugar!"

Jean picked up the recipe card and looked at it. "Well!" she exclaimed. "Who would have thought that two cups of sugar could make such a difference?"

A whole cherry pie—ruined!

"Oh no!" I exclaimed. "What are we going to do?"

"Perhaps we could dress in rags and beg outside a bakery," Jack suggested. We threw our three pieces away.

"Would you be serious?"

Just then we heard a dog barking outside. I went into the dining room and looked outside the sliding glass door. Bruno was back.

"What's he doing here?" I asked Jack. Jack shrugged. "He likes me, I guess," he replied.

"Could we slide the back door open?" Jean asked. "I'm hot."

"Me, too," Jack called, pulling the first batch of apple turnovers out of the oven.

It *was* hot in the kitchen. I pulled back the sliding glass door. Bruno came up to the screen and slobbered on it hopefully. "Would you go away?" I asked him. He wagged his tail. Bruno's owners grumble at Bruno so much that he thinks that's how everybody talks. He barked invitingly.

I turned around and walked away. As I did, there was a colossal ripping noise behind me—that distinctive sound of screen ripping. I spun around and got knocked over by two hundred pounds of gregarious wolfhound.

"Jack!" I screamed.

Barking gleefully, Bruno snapped at the dangling tablecloth to pull it down.

Even Jack was horrified, and Jean was crying by this time.

"Go home!" he yelled at the dog. "Go home!" He started flinging apple turnovers at Bruno, hailing the dog with pastries which—I couldn't help noticing—had been baked as hard as bricks. Bruno turned tail and fled to the living room, yelping.

I sat up and looked at the ruin of turnovers everywhere, the screen door ripped from top to bottom, and the tablecloth pulled almost all the way to the floor. Fortunately, the plates had only slid, not fallen off. Nothing was broken. I looked at the time. 10:25.

"Oh, Jack! What will we do!" I yelled. Jean was so surprised that she stopped crying just to look at me.

And then the door bell rang. "That's them!" I cried. "A half hour early! The Ladies' Auxiliary Missionary Fellowship has come to judge us, and we're doomed!"

Jack went and answered the door. Sure enough, it was Mrs. Bennett and Miss Crumble, two of the little old ladies.

"Would you believe," I heard Jack say, "that you're at the wrong house? The Derwoods that you're looking for moved away last week."

"We heard about your poor mother's accident," Miss Crumble began, laughing at his feeble joke, "and we came to help out." She must have realized that things were going badly.

"Oh, Jack!" I sobbed. "Bring them in!"

"Now that's what I call the response of a true missionary!" Mrs. Bennett exclaimed, as she and Miss Crumble came in. Mrs. Bennett had a cherry pie in her hands. I stood up. "Oh, my!" she exclaimed softly. "Were you having a pillow fight?"

"A dogfight," I replied.

She took the whole situation in and made sense out of it somehow.

"I believe," she said to Miss Crumble, "that I will take command in the kitchen."

"I read you," Miss Crumble said. "I'll take the dining room. Come on, Penny," she said briskly. "You can help me."

Miss Crumble was thin and straight and cheerful. She laughed at the screen door until she had tears in her eyes, and when she saw the turnovers lying around and heard how Jack chased Bruno out, she had to sit down while I finished straightening the plates. I never saw anybody laugh so hard. She used her boot laces to tie together the jagged parts of the screen, and then we closed the sliding glass door.

I could hear Bruno galloping around the kitchen, barking and whining for Mrs. Bennett to pay attention to him. I figured he would be knocking her over in a minute.

"Don't worry about the dog," Miss Crumble kept saying as we straightened the table setting. "Marie loves dogs."

I tried to explain how Bruno reacted to people; then all of a sudden I realized he wasn't barking any more. That scared me even more. I dashed into the kitchen.

"What's he doing?" I cried. Then I stopped. He was just standing there—sort of puzzled—licking his chops over and over again.

"Peanut butter," Mrs. Bennett said. "It works every time. They love it. Come on, Bruno," and she shooed him out the kitchen door. I looked at her with new admiration. Anybody smart enough to stick peanut butter on the roof of a dog's mouth—especially Bruno's—really did know dogs. There was more to Mrs. Bennett than I had thought. Was this the same lady that got so teary-eyed at weddings?

She went back to consoling Jean and let her help make a new batch of apple turnovers. And she set Jack to brewing coffee.

"Just make it very strong, Jack," she told him. "Miss Banks likes it strong—and I mean strong." She raised her eyebrows.

"I'm going to get the gear, Marie," Miss Crumble said to Mrs. Bennett.

"Gear?" I asked. Mrs. Bennett thrust a dishtowel into my hands.

"Miss Crumble is our photographer," she said.

In a minute Miss Crumble came back in, a tripod over one shoulder and a camera case slung around her neck. "I'd like to get a shot of that wolfhound first," she said. "Good, dark fur against the snow."

"Better take some peanut butter," Mrs. Bennett warned.

"Right."

I glanced at the clock. 10:55. The dining room was put back together, and Mrs. Bennett would oversee the pie and turnovers. I meant to tell her that we had ruined the first pie, but just then somebody knocked.

"Bring them in!" Mrs. Bennett called cheerfully.

A short, stocky woman entered. "Smells like coffee!" she boomed. "Bring me a cup, sonny, would you?" she asked Jack.

"Miss Banks!" Mrs. Bennett exclaimed pleasantly.

"I was almost late, Marie, playing out in the snow with the kids," she exclaimed. "Wow, but it's great to have snow! Built a nice little fort and slicked it down last night. This morning it was froze solid. I held off four fifth-graders and two baby-sitters! Yup. Thank you, sonny!" She took the coffee cup from Jack and swallowed most of it all at once. "My lands! That's the best coffee I've had in months! Can I have another?"

He got her another. She sat down on a kitchen chair. "Your mouth is open, honey!" she exclaimed at me. I hurriedly shut my mouth, and she started laughing. She called me a likely girl. "Say!" she added. "Where's Alice? Her car's out there."

"She's getting a picture of a wolfhound playing in the snow," Mrs. Bennett said.

"A wolfhound! I haven't played with a dog that big in years!" She drained her coffee and stumped out the back way.

I glanced at Jack. "Miss Banks served in World War II," Mrs. Bennett said lightly, noticing the look. "We like to have her speak because she has so many interesting stories to tell."

"A girl soldier?" Jack asked.

"A WAAC," she explained. "She was a nurse in the Women's Army Auxiliary Corps. It was a dangerous job for her. She often worked close to the front. Then she was moved to Africa right at the end. She went back as a missionary. That's why she likes snow so much. She went a long time without it."

Soon the other ladies came. We had about ten in all. I went out with Jack to take coats and make conversation. Jean was helping Miss Crumble set up her equipment in the dining room. When I came back into the kitchen, Mrs. Bennett had cut up the new cherry pie and dished it out on little dessert plates. The pieces of new pie were mixed in with the old pie. My heart sank.

Jack and Jean came in and saw it. "All I can do," Jack began, "is make a solemn vow to eat as much cherry pie as possible in the hopes of getting the bad pieces first."

Long before anybody else had finished her sandwich, Jack brought out the desserts on a big tray. The three of us started on cherry pie. There were thirteen pieces, and five were bad.

Jack got a head start on me while I finished my sandwich. Soon I saw him hold up three fingers. So he was already on his third bad one. In a way we could figure out which were the bad pieces because we had cut our pie with a blunt knife. I found one piece that looked pretty mangled. It was bad, all right. Jean looked at me very tearfully and nodded her head. She had the last bad one. I breathed a sigh of relief as I took a few more bites.

Afterwards Miss Banks stood up and gave her testimony, and she told us a lot of war stories in it. I got so wrapped up in it that I forgot about Jack and the pie. But just as Miss Banks was getting to an exciting part about an air raid and tramping boots, she stopped talking and stared hard across the table.

"Lands! That boy's going to fa—"

Before she got it out, Jack very slowly toppled sideways off his chair.

"Jack!" I screamed.

"The pies!" Jean cried, and burst into tears again.

I ran to his side. "Jack, are you all right?" He was groaning.

"Step back, honey. I'm a nurse," Miss Banks told me.

"Oh, Penny," Jack groaned. "When you call the ambulance, don't forget the fire station is fifty dollars cheaper than the rescue squad."

"Nobody said anything about fire or rescue, sonny," Miss Banks said. "From the way you put away all that pie—"

He groaned louder.

"I wouldn't mention it just now," I suggested.

"Well, help me lift him then," she said.

After we got Jack to his bed, I told them what had happened to the first cherry pie and why Jack had eaten so much.

"Well, he'll live," Miss Banks said sternly, but her grey eyes were twinkling. "No sugar indeed! Three pieces!"

Miss Crumble was turning red. I knew she wanted to laugh but was holding it in. "Lands, I'm about to pop my pearls," she whimpered, and went out back. Even through the glass door and the curtains, I could hear her laughing.

Mrs. Bennett helped everybody with coats and hats, and the Ladies' Auxiliary Missionary Fellowship Annual Luncheon was over. She and Jean and I cleaned up. When we next checked on Jack, he was still white as a sheet, but at least he was asleep.

I promised Mrs. Bennett that I would watch out for him, and then she left, too.

Much later that afternoon he woke up. He looked healthy again. He lifted his head and grinned.

"Hey," he said weakly. "Look who's sitting by my bed! Do you make house calls free of charge?"

"Jack, you're the greatest brother in the world," I said. "Even if everything went wrong today—you were great!"

"A deputy does his duty." He lay back and smiled. "I'll tell you what I never knew," he said softly, "how dangerous a Ladies' Auxiliary Missionary Fellowship Annual Luncheon could be!"

We both burst out laughing. "Next year," he said with a sigh, "we'll serve popcorn for dessert. It's cheaper, too."

I made him tea a little later on. Then Jean came upstairs and read her report about Columbus to him, which he listened to patiently. He was trying to be better with her since I'd given him a lecture about how often she felt left out.

After I'd gotten the kids fed and put to bed, I exercised Harry the Hamster for a while. Harry was starting to get pretty ferocious about being awakened every two hours. Jack was slipping him coffee drops in his water and exercising him often to prevent him from hibernating.

Then at last Dad came home from the hospital and said that Mom had hurt herself worse than the paramedics had thought and that it might be a while until she came home. But he told me not to worry, it would just be a few weeks, and then he kissed me good night.

"I do have some good news," he told me, smiling.

"What, Dad?"

He slipped a receipt into my hand. On it were the words

ONE SMUGGLERS' MATTRESS
PAID IN FULL.

ELEVEN

DERWOOD UNINCORPORATES

"Penny, you've got to learn to cook," Jack said soberly.

"I can't, Jack. I don't have time."

"Penny, I will take over doing the laundry if you will only learn how to cook."

"I don't think I could without Mom here."

"Penny, I will make the supreme sacrifice for you. I, Jack Derwood, the eleven-year-old most often mistaken for Ebenezer Scrooge, will *pay* you to learn how to cook. And if you ruin any of Mom's pots or pans, I'll buy new ones for you."

He let his hamburger drop into its wrapper. It landed with a flabby flop. Next to Jack, across the table from me, Jean sighed and nodded. Freddy, Renee, and Marie looked hopefully at me.

"Could we have spaghetti tomorrow night?" Freddy asked hopefully.

"Freddy, you know I don't know how to make spaghetti. I only know how to bake."

"Let's have apple pie then!" Marie exclaimed.

"Quit bugging me! We can't have pie for dinner, and I don't have time before tomorrow night to learn how to cook anything else!"

Jack almost answered back, and there would have been a big argument, but he caught himself all of a sudden. "Okay," he answered, letting little Marie climb into his lap. She glanced at me reproachfully. "Penny's mean," she said, her mouth, still babyishly round, stuck out from pouting.

"Mean, mean, mean—" Freddy and Renee began to chant.

Jack suddenly straightened. "That's enough, you guys. It's not fair to make Penny do everything. Stop it." Freddy and Renee stopped, a little surprised at having Jack tell them what to do. "We promised Dad we wouldn't fight," he added quickly, before they could argue. "And it's dumb to call people names. I call for a thirty-second Think. On your mark, get set, go!"

Marie slid back into her chair. Everybody stuck their elbows on the table and frowned fiercely into space. Thinks were Jack's idea. He was the only person who called for them, and he usually used them to get the younger ones to do what he wanted them to.

"Time's up!" he exclaimed. "Freddy, it's your turn to speak first. What do we do about dinner tomorrow night?"

"Let Dad buy us hamburgers again."

"All in favor say aye," Jack called. Nobody stirred.

"Okay, Freddy, you have to go take your bath now— you're out."

Freddy sighed, slid off his chair, and left. Jack went up the line. Jean suggested waiting for Aunt Miriam. She had gone to Florida before Mom's accident and wouldn't be back from vacation for two weeks. She didn't even know about Mom's fall yet. But two weeks was a long time for us to wait, so Jack decreed Jean's suggestion to be impractical. She was assigned to do the few dishes we'd used, and Renee and Marie were assigned to clean up the living room when they in their turns failed to think of anything.

"This is called an impasse," he said, looking at me. He pronounced it *impassey*. "Do you have a suggestion?"

"Yeah, *you* cook dinner tomorrow night."

"Good idea." He suddenly straightened and looked out the window. "Hey, there's Dad, and it's still light outside. The deacons' meeting must have ended extra early. We could go up to the store now if you wanted."

"For what?" I asked.

"To get some stuff for me to cook dinner tomorrow night. That's what you suggested, wasn't it?"

"Now, Jack—" The Ladies' Auxiliary Missionary Fellowship Annual Luncheon was still fresh in my mind.

"Come on, let's go ask him!" Jack urged. I wasn't quite sure, but hamburgers were getting to be awfully monotonous after two weeks. I knew that at least whatever Jack made would be entertaining, so I gave in and followed him.

"Jack, Penny," Dad said. "I—" He stopped and looked blank. "I, uh—"

"What is it Dad?" I asked.

"Uh, uh, your mother wants you to return the silver to Mrs. Bennett. Mom borrowed it from her a week ago for the Ladies' Auxiliary Luncheon. She's worried about our having something that's worth so much money in the house. Mrs. Bennett inherited it from her grandmother, and it's very valuable. Your mother would feel terrible if it were to be stolen while we were all out of the house."

"It's still light outside. We could run it up to her house now, if you like," I said.

"Could we run up to the quick mart, too?" Jack asked.

"What son? Oh, sure," Dad said. He seemed even more absent-minded than usual as he fumbled with his billfold. "Need groceries again? Well, I guess we would. You and your sister are managing very well."

"Did you see Mom today?" I asked. Kids could only go on Saturdays to visit at the hospital. But Dad went every day.

"Yes, I was just with her. You'd better get the silver now."

Jack took the money and grabbed my hand. "Come on, Penny."

I turned to look at Dad as Jack pulled me away. "What about the deacons' meeting? Didn't you go?"

He wasn't listening, and as Jack dragged me away, I realized that something was wrong. Dad had to tell us something. But he was putting it off.

We went into the dining room and gathered together all the silver: teaspoons, serving forks, and spreading knives. "They sure are pretty," I said as I held a spoon under the dining room lamp. It looked almost pure white in the light.

"Mom must have had a box for it," Jack said, looking through the china cabinet. "Where'd she hide it?"

"Oh, we better not take the time to try to find it," I said. "Come on." I went into the kitchen and rolled the silver up snugly in one of Mom's spacious aprons. The apron strings were long enough to be crisscrossed over the long bundle to hold it securely, knotted, and then tied around my own waist. I put my jacket on to hide the bulge. That way my hands were free. All I had to do was keep one hand over the rolled-up apron to make sure it was okay.

When Dad saw it, he raised an eyebrow. "That's how house burglars hide silver when they steal it," he said. "You two haven't been investigating any robberies, have you?" And he laughed at his own joke, like he was trying to be light-hearted.

"No. 'Bye, Dad," I called.

"Let's go," Jack said. "We have to hurry! We may have to run part of the way!"

"I don't think I can run with this thing around me," I called as I dashed out of the house after him.

"I'll make soup," Jack was saying when I caught up with him. "Jack Derwood's Soup du Jour! That's 'soup of the day' in German. All us great cooks know that."

"It's French," I told him. "Did Dad seem worried to you?"

"Dad always seems worried when Mom's not here," he replied. "Let's cut across the field."

"Okay."

"We'd better run."

"I'll try."

I did try, too, but the apron kept banging here and there inside my jacket, and it felt loose, so I had to stop. "Jack, wait!" I yelled. Night was coming fast, and I didn't like to be alone in the wide field between the back of the quick mart and our neighborhood.

Jack came back. "I'll take it for you," he said.

"I think it's coming loose," I warned him.

"Oh, it'll hold until we get to Mrs. Bennett's house."
He tied it around his waist and tugged his jacket over
it. "I just hope nobody notices I've got an apron on
in here."

"It's rolled up. Pretend it's a money belt."

"Hah! Now that's something I'd like to have!" He
buttoned the two bottom buttons of his jacket over it so
that the jacket would look loose and natural and still
cover the apron. But the rolled-up apron still managed
to bulge out a little. "How do burglars do it, Penny?
They walk around with TVs and refrigerators under
their coats and nobody notices," he said, looking down
at the bulge in puzzlement. "And why would burglars
steal silverware, anyway? Is it worth a lot?"

"It is if it's real silver, like this stuff is. Carry it in
your hand if it bothers you around your waist."

"No. We have to carry the groceries back. I'm sure
we'll need two bags if we have to lug them to Mrs.
Bennett's and then back home. One full bag might
break. Come on. It's getting dark."

We trudged through the long field of tall grass that
backed up on the quick mart. Jack was immersed in
planning the soup he was going to make for us and
trying to keep the apron full of silver from slipping, and
I was worried about Dad, so we came around to the
front without noticing much, like the broken glass all
over the sidewalk and the two police cars out in front of
the quick mart.

Then somebody yelled, "There they are! They did
it! They did it!" And a big policeman came walking
over to us.

Jack was quick. "What's going on?" he asked.

"Scruggs Grady!" I exclaimed. That was the kid yelling at us. If we had been on the street, I would have been scared, but in front of the lighted store with two policemen there, I wasn't.

"Hey," the nearer policeman said gruffly. "What do you two know about this window?"

"What window?" Jack asked. I could have kicked him for looking so blank in front of Scruggs.

"The store window," I hissed in his car. "It's broken!"

The two policemen came closer, arms folded across their chests.

"The cashier says two kids ran up and heaved a rock through his window," one of them said. "You two know anything about it?"

"No, officer," Jack said. "We just got here. We're buying groceries."

"They threw the rock," Scruggs yelled, "and hid behind the store until they thought you were gone! I saw them!"

"You're a liar, Scruggs Grady!" I yelled back.

"Look," Jack said. "My dad just got home, and he sent us to the store. You can call him—or—" Here he had a sudden inspiration. "Ask Sergeant McKenna. He goes to our church. He knows us, and he knows we wouldn't do anything like that."

"Well," the big officer said, rubbing his chin. "McKenna's on his way over here now. What do you think of that?"

"That's fine," Jack said, and I nodded. But I wondered how we would explain the silver to the police if they should happen to notice the bulge in Jack's jacket. The night cashier from the store came outside.

"You recognize these two?" the bigger policeman asked him.

"They sure look like they could be the ones," he said.

"Can we help it if we were born with dishonest faces?" Jack asked.

"Be quiet, Jack," I whispered. Jack didn't mean to be rude, but he always kept talking when he was nervous.

"My sister here is ashamed of it, as you can see. But I figure there's good business in looking like a crook. I mean, think of the job opportunities. Why, I could pose for wanted posters or—"

Then I saw why he was nervous. The apron was slipping! Sure enough, the bulge was settling lower and lower in his jacket. He was trying to keep it pinned in with his arms while seeming to be relaxed. And he was talking on and on so nobody would notice the bulge.

"—or I could go undercover, like in the upholstery business. Make slipcovers by day and break up spy rings at night, an undercover slipcover agent—"

A voice interrupted us. "Is that Jack Derwood running his mouth again?" Frank McKenna strode under the neon and fluorescent lights of the quick mart. "What's all this about, kids?" I felt so relieved that I broke out into a sweat. I hadn't even noticed him driving up.

"You been practicing baseball with rocks?" he asked us.

Jack was nearly groaning with the strain of trying to keep the apron stuffed with silver pinned to his waist with just his wrists. One apron string was dangling from under his jacket, but it was in the back.

I answered, "We just got here, Mr. McKenna, and that kid Scruggs Grady said we broke the window, but we didn't. We left our house less than twenty minutes ago."

He nodded, real cool and calm and turned to the cops. "These kids are okay. This is Jack and Penny Derwood. Where's the boy who said—?" They turned to look for Scruggs, but he had vanished.

"See?" I demanded triumphantly.

"Well, of course," the cashier said, embarrassed. "I've seen these two plenty of times. And I read about them, too. I didn't recognize them there for a minute under the lights and all."

Then the other two policemen remembered us. They were township police and hadn't been as close to the smuggling case as the local Peabody police.

Sergeant McKenna grinned at us and shrugged. "Sorry kids. Didn't mean to scare you."

Jack was really straining to keep the apron hidden, and I could see that both of the apron strings were dangling from under the back of his jacket.

"S'okay," I said, moving to cover him. "We've got to go."

"Can I give you a ride back home?" he asked.

"No, no, that's all right." I nudged Jack along, trying to help hide the dangling string and the bulge.

But we had to get past Sergeant McKenna to get into the store. "Okay," he said. "I'll see you two in church." And he gave Jack a hearty slap on the back. Jack jumped, startled, and a cascade of sterling silver dropped to the sidewalk.

*   *   *   *   *   *

"Oh, hi, Dad," Jack said when Dad came to pick us up at the police station. "What are you in for?"

"Jack," Dad began, sounding tired and not ready for any jokes.

"I'm awful sorry, Mr. Derwood," Sergeant McKenna said quickly. "When we called Mrs. Bennett, she verified their story. Still, it was official procedure to bring them here first."

Dad waved it away. "It's all right. For myself, I don't know many kids who would have a good reason for carrying around a bunch of sterling silver tied up in an apron, either." He suddenly smiled. "Besides, who could trust a mug like that?" and he tousled Jack's hair. So he wasn't angry.

"How's the wife?" the sergeant asked.

"Well, not good. We thought that injury to her hip would be slight, but there are back problems now. She might—" But then he caught himself as he glanced at us. "Well, the doctors have some tests to run yet. Come on kids. Let's go home."

Jack and I were silent in the car; then I said, "Who's home with the kids, Dad?"

He glanced down at me. "Annette's mother."

We nodded.

"How about some ice cream, kids?" Dad asked.

"Sure!" Jack exclaimed. "This busting out of jail isn't half bad!"

We pulled in at a restaurant and went in. After we had ordered our sundaes, Dad said, "Penny, Jack, do you remember your Aunt Irene?"

Jack brightened. "Yeah! The real mean aunt? The one who's Mom's oldest sister?"

"Yeah, the one Mom was always afraid of when they were growing up," I put in. Mom has eleven brothers and sisters, but they are scattered all over the country. "Aunt Irene was the one who cornered that gangster in the shed. She kept him backed into the corner with a broom until the police came."

"Oh, yeah, and isn't she the one that Mom said chased the neighbor's German shepherd around the block three times before he rolled over and pretended to be dead? Boy, what a mean woman!" Jack laughed.

"Kids in Mom's neighborhood used to say that dairy farmers would hire Aunt Irene to curdle their milk for them to make cheese," I told Jack. "She used to make Mom and the other brothers and sisters take cod liver oil."

The waitress brought our sundaes. Jack slapped his knee. "That's right! And she knocked out her eighth-grade teacher when he said she was cheating on a test!" He looked up at Dad. "What about her, Dad?"

"Yeah." I turned to him. "What's up with Aunt Irene, Dad?"

Dad cleared his throat and looked down at his sundae. "You're spending the summer with her, Penny."

Jack's jaw dropped into his whipped cream.

TWELVE

SCRUGGS

Summer and the doom of Aunt Irene's was still a month away. Jack tried to console me, but I felt pretty miserable. For some reason Aunt Irene had actually *offered* to take me in order to help Mom and Dad out. I got an idea from the way Dad talked to her over the phone that Aunt Irene considered one of me equal to a whole batch of other kids. My reputation had preceded me.

Aunt Miriam would soon keep house while Mom was in therapy for her back. Mom still had to stay in the hospital for awhile.

Meanwhile, Annette was up to her old "you're adopted" routine, which she pulled whenever Jack and I weren't around Jean and the littler ones to shoo her off or change the subject. And we *still* hadn't returned Mrs. Bennett's silver. The Ladies' Auxiliary Missionary Fellowship Annual Luncheon had been weeks ago.

"We'd better take it to her," Jack said one Saturday. "Now if we got arrested for stealing silver, we wouldn't have much defense—we've kept it so long. Come on."

He had found the box for it, so we trudged up the street to the next block.

There was a ten-speed bicycle parked outside Mrs. Bennett's small house.

"Who could this belong to?" Jack wondered.

"Maybe she's got company from church," I guessed as I knocked.

She answered the door a minute later.

"Oh, Jack and Penny! Come in!" she said, stepping aside.

"We brought your silver," Jack said, offering her the box.

"Thank you. I've had an apple pie cooling while William mowed my back yard for me. Why not stay and have some?"

We didn't know who William was; there was nobody at church by that name, but we hadn't been eating too well lately, and Aunt Miriam wouldn't be coming until Monday. We said yes and thank you and followed her into her small kitchen.

And there, right at her table, was Scruggs Grady. Jack gasped. So did I.

"Oh, you know each other," Mrs. Bennett said.

Scruggs looked up and—of all things—turned red when he saw us.

"*Know* him?" Jack asked. "He tried twice to make me eat a worm, and he's been pickin' on me and—say, what's up with you, anyway?" he demanded of Scruggs. "What are you doing here? You'd better leave Mrs. Bennett—"

"Jack—" Mrs. Bennett's voice stopped him. "William has been cutting my yard for me, and he's my guest— just as you are."

That last part was a pointed reminder to behave like a guest, but Jack was sure that Scruggs was out to take advantage of Mrs. Bennett's kindness without her knowing it.

"Oh, you don't know this kid. He's always picking on us. He picks on everybody. He'd pick on you if you weren't a—a—" He almost said "old lady," but he caught himself just in time. Jack blushed and turned to Scruggs. "What are you after, anyway? Whyn't you say something? Can't talk without your pals?"

"Jack!" Mrs. Bennett came around the stove. I felt embarrassed, but I was sure she just didn't understand we were trying to let her know the truth about Scruggs.

"*Will* you mind your manners and behave?" she asked Jack. "I've already told you that William is my guest."

"I guess I better go then," Jack replied, so sullenly that he even surprised me. "I won't sit down with that bully. Thanks anyway for the pie. Come on, Penny."

And he stalked out.

I didn't know what to say—seemed like we were being rude, but I stammered, "I'd better go, too." And I followed him.

We walked down the driveway and then up the block.

"Boy," he said at last. "Are we going to get in trouble now."

"Yeah—if she tells Dad, but maybe she won't. Maybe she'll bawl us out herself after church tomorrow," I said, and then added, "and that won't be much better."

"I'd like to know where that mug gets off, mooching pie from her."

"You know Mrs. Bennett. She's soft-hearted," I told him. "Scruggs gave her some hard-luck story, and now she feels sorry for him."

Then we walked on in silence mostly, but every now and then we'd spit out some comment about Scruggs and what we thought of him.

On top of all that, we got home to find that Annette had been visiting. Marie was in tears. She ran and hugged me. "What's 'adopted'?" she asked. "Why does it make everybody cry?"

"Has somebody been telling you you're adopted?" I asked, lifting her up.

Jack was really seething by this time. He found Freddy and Renee. Jean, who had supposedly been watching the kids, had been upstairs doing homework. She came downstairs when she heard us. I think Jack would have yelled at her for leaving Annette with the little ones, but I interrupted him. "We need a plan," I said.

"Yeah?" Jack stopped seething long enough to look interested.

"Sure. Marie, don't you know what adopted means?" I asked her. She shook her head and leaned it against me. "What if I told you it means that you get to eat ice cream?" I asked her.

Everybody perked up at that.

"It doesn't mean that," she laughed, shaking her head but then eyeing me with hope.

"It could," I said. "And it could also mean getting to wear a patch on your jacket and being in your own club."

"Why?" she asked.

"Yeah, why?" Jean echoed.

"Well, the way I see it, we always get mad by denying it over and over again to Annette when she's standing there smirking and saying we're adopted. So let's not deny it. Let's all be convinced. Every Derwood in this room is hereby ordered to 'fall for it,' so to speak."

"What will that prove?" Jack asked.

"That orphans have more fun," I said. "It's time we did our own smirking. Why don't you and Jean go find some red scraps in Mom's scrapbag? Then when we form our Orphans Only Club, we can all have matching patches."

Well, everybody liked the idea of having a club of our own, so they all went to the scrapbag. I sketched out two *O*s right next to each other like spectacles.

Jean got scissors and needles and thread. She and I were the only two who could do any real sewing. We let the little ones pick scraps while Jack did the tracing and cutting. First we hemmed the patches along their outside edges, and then we sewed them onto our jackets.

As it turned out, we didn't have enough of any one material to make all six patches. Jean and Freddy got solid red. Marie, Renee, and I got red with tiny black polka dots, and Jack got red with little white birds on it. He wanted two patches after that, so he could wear them like the epaulets of a general, but my fingers were too sore, so I told him no.

Jean had the idea to include Sherwood in the club. Mrs. Bennett had given us Sherwood from a litter of kittens that her cat Clair had given birth to. Clair had died soon after. So Jean thought that we should include Sherwood as an orphan, too, and we could sew her a little cape with the patch on the back. At first that sounded like a good idea, but then we realized that Harry the Hamster was also an orphan—we presumed his parents had died in hibernation long ago—and there was no way I was going to sew him a cape and try

to get it onto him. So in the end we voted to exclude animals from the club.

We ate a late lunch, and then Dad came and took us to see Mom, who was doing pretty well in therapy.

We got home around six o'clock, just in time to catch the ice-cream man driving by and ringing his bell.

Jack ordered six nutty buddies while we ran inside to slip into our jackets. We hurried back outside and sat in a line on the curb, from oldest to youngest, having a contest to see who could make his cone last the longest.

Pretty soon, Annette came along.

"What are you doing?" she asked.

"Sitting on the curb," Jack told her.

She stood there a minute, shifting her weight from foot to foot, wondering why we were all together like that. At last she said, "Wanna' play kickball?"

"No, we're busy," Jack said.

She looked at him with a frown. "Busy doing what?"

"Sitting on the curb."

"Why?"

He showed her the patch on his shoulder. "Training," he said. "Adopted kids have to be good at sitting on the curb looking forlorn."

"You don't look forlorn to me."

"That part comes next week. Can't take on too much training at once."

She shifted and looked unhappy. "This is silly."

"You just don't understand. You see, you're *not* adopted."

"What does a pair of spectacles on your sleeve have to do with being adopted?"

"Those aren't spectacles," I retorted. "They're two capital *O*s O.O.—Orphans Only. That's our club name."

"Can I join?"

"Are you adopted?" I asked pointedly. And there I had her, because she knew if she gave in and pretended she was, we would be forever reminding her of it in the future when she teased any of us.

"Are *you?*" she demanded.

I didn't know what to say because we really weren't, but Jack spoke up. "You say we are. So we're giving in. Agreeing. Accepting the facts."

Boy, she really looked sore when she realized her favorite joke had backfired, but I could see she was determined not to give in and say we weren't adopted. She knew we would always remind her of that, too. So she stalked off in a huff.

We sat on the curb until dark.

After church on Sunday Mrs. Bennett found us. She looked kind of sorry and disappointed in us. "I was sorry to see how you reacted to Will Grady on Saturday," she said gently.

Jack huffed out his breath.

"Mrs. Bennett," I said. "Scruggs has been picking on us for years. You don't know all the things he's done to us—"

"I *do* know."

Well, I told myself she did not, either, but I couldn't contradict her out loud. She must have read my thoughts.

"Oh, Penny, William told me himself!" she exclaimed. "Couldn't you see how miserable he was when you and Jack accused him to his face? If you had offered him one hope of forgiving him, he would have been your friend forever."

Jack started a little bit at her words. Because, of course, she made it sound like we had wronged Scruggs.

"Will has been working for me for several weeks," she told us. "He's a troubled boy. He needs friends now."

"He could *always* have made friends with us," Jack said. "Even if he is older, we'd have been friends with him, but he's a bully."

She gathered her things to leave. "You two don't understand his position. Not every child has somebody to tell him right from wrong while he's growing up, or someone to protect him from being hurt. If you had only forgiven him on Saturday, you would have proved Christianity to him."

Jack walked away, pretending to be mad, but I saw the unexpected flush on his cheeks, and I knew that really he was ashamed of himself.

"Have you been witnessing to Scruggs?" I asked. She nodded. "For a long time. I won't give up hope for him."

I felt as mean and rotten as Jack did. But there wasn't anything we could say to each other.

On Monday after school we had to wait for Aunt Miriam to come, and that wouldn't be for several hours. We decided to play kickball down at the ball field, and we were still in such a contrite mood that we asked Annette to join us, but she was still sulking about Orphans Only and how we had made such a joke about her joke. She told us that she wouldn't play with us until we took those patches off.

Jack liked his patch too much and was still hoping for epaulets, so he said no.

Then she got really mad and said, "You just wait, Jack and Penny Derwood. I'm going to advertise your silly club, and you're going to have another member pretty soon!"

Well, that didn't frighten us. We all put on our jackets and trooped down to the ball field.

We got a game going—Jack, Freddy, and Marie against me, Jean, and Renee. We just kept playing until one team had twenty-one points.

It was about the sixteenth inning, and Jack was pitching to Jean, when I saw somebody come out from the hedge and walk across the field toward us. I realized it was Scruggs.

"Jack," I said. He turned to see Scruggs, and I looked around, but I didn't see any of Scruggs's cronies skulking around. At the sight of us Scruggs stopped, and I could see him counting heads and figuring out that everybody playing was a Derwood. He hesitated as though doubtful of coming up or leaving. Suddenly Jack gave me one glance and yelled, "You wanna play?"

Then he came up, cracking his knuckles.

"I, uh, got a phone call," he said. "About some group of kids from your church—is there anybody else coming out here to play ball?"

"Just us," Jack told him. We weren't afraid of Scruggs when there was a bunch of us and he was alone, but we stood there, kind of awkward. Then I slowly realized what Annette had done. Scruggs's real parents were dead. She had advertised us to him as a *bona fide* club. He had come to join up. Jack had already realized this because he was standing with his left side to Scruggs so that he wouldn't see the patch. The last thing anybody wanted to do was make Scruggs mad unnecessarily. But then I felt sorry for him, too. He had come looking to join up with kids he thought he had something in common with, and it was all just a joke—a mean joke.

"Scruggs," I said. "I'm sorry for what I did on Saturday. And you can play kickball with us if you want."

"Yeah," Jack said. "Me, too. We'll start a new game and choose up new sides. If anybody else comes along, we'll just add them to the smaller team. How's that?"

Scruggs looked at the ground, then at his shoes. "Okay," he said.

THIRTEEN

THE DESPERATE ESCAPADE OF HARRY THE HAMSTER

Our train pulled out one morning. We waved to Dad and Aunt Miriam and the kids and then settled down to await our doom.

"Jack, I'm glad you're coming with me. I'm scared."

"You don't have anything to be glad about," he said. "I'm scared, too—more than you." Suddenly he jumped a little, jerked his hand out of his left jacket pocket, and then stuffed it back in. I stared, but he acted like nothing was wrong.

"Why us?" I moaned. "Why us?"

He sighed. "Because we're deputies. We knew this job would be dangerous when we took it."

He was silent a moment, then became serious. "Dad had to let us go, Penny. Six of us were too much—that's a lot of cooking on Aunt Miriam, and the little ones need to be close to Mom so that they can visit her at least once a week." Then he jumped again like something electrical had shocked him, but he didn't say anything.

"And what if the doctors have her moved to that special hospital in Ohio?" I asked.

"Then at least they'll be with Dad. But you and I are older, and we're not supposed to mind." He looked out the window of the train. The rolling Wisconsin landscape had at last given way to more uneven land. Soon we would be traveling through mountains. Dad had said that Aunt Irene lived in a little city close to where the Allegheny and the Blue Ridge mountains met. The thought of Aunt Irene sent another rush of dread over me. I was grateful to have Jack with me. He had begged Dad to let him come, too. At long last, after a month of Dad asking over the phone, Aunt Irene had agreed. But she said she disapproved of "gimcracks," and we'd better have them all out of our system by the time we reached her house. That had scared Jack because he didn't know what gimcracks were, and the word wasn't in our dictionary. Dad told us that Aunt Irene meant we had better behave. But I'd thought we had been behaving.

"I don't know how to thank you for coming, Jack," I said at last.

"I'll write a list," he said quickly and laughed, embarrassed. Then he asked, "Do you pray for Mom, Penny?"

"Of course I do!"

"Every day, I mean."

"Well, almost every day. I try to make it every day." Mom and Dad had always been careful to make sure we had devotions every day, but with Mom still in the hospital and Dad trying to look after everything, Dad sometimes forgot to ask us or wasn't home to see to it. Every time I thought about Mom, I asked God to bring her home and make her back and hip all right again, but I didn't count that as devotions. And sometimes a whole day went by with my being too busy to worry about her.

"I try to pray for her every day, too," he said. He squirmed in his seat. "While we're at—uh—Aunt Irene's—" he began. "What I mean is, if things get rough this summer—I don't want to preach at you, and I hate it when people pray *at* each other, but I think it would be good, and Dad said so, too—"

"What?" I asked.

"I think we should pray together every day this summer," he said quickly, "and I promise I won't pray at you."

I nodded. "Okay, and I won't pray at you, either."

A long time ago in family devotions when it was my turn to pray out loud, I used to say things like, "Please show Jack that it's a sin to crack his knuckles, and let him know what a rude and disgusting habit it is."

That's what we called "praying at" somebody, and it continued until Dad pointed out to us that we were turning the family altar into a family court. He told us that we were really making our prayers an excuse to say whatever we felt like saying, and that was blasphemy.

"Praying at" each other had been outlawed in family devotions, but every now and then somebody would try to slip it in. So I had never felt comfortable praying with my brothers and sisters unless Dad was there to referee.

Suddenly Jack jumped again and pulled his hand out of his pocket. He looked away, shaking his hand, and then thrust it back in.

"Jack," I said.

He glanced up at the luggage rack. "Hmm?" Then—uncontrollably—he twitched again.

"What's wrong with you?" I asked.

"What do you mean what's wrong with me? Eeyow!" He pulled his hand free again and shook his fingers.

"What have you got in your pocket?"

He glanced at his right pocket. "Nothing."

"In your *other* pocket."

"Shhhh. Keep your voice down," he whispered. He glanced furtively around, then looked down at his left pocket, and very gingerly put his hand into it. Once again he jumped, but he managed to suppress the jump into a quiver. After a small struggle he pulled something out, something that peeped out of his hand with two gleaming eyes.

"Harry!" I cried. Jack shushed me, and then surveyed the hamster proudly. "He's two years and four months old today," he said.

Harry, however, was anything but pleased with his longevity. He clashed his grinders and struggled to bite the hand that held him.

"I don't get him," Jack said irritably as he tried to cradle the ferocious hamster on his lap. "Here he is, still alive into his third year, and he hates me. You'd think he'd figure out I'm trying to save his life."

"Dad says Harry doesn't want to live forever; he just wants to sleep."

"How could he? I thought all animals wanted to live."

"Cheer up. He doesn't hate you especially. He hates everyone." Only two days before, Sherwood the cat had figured out how to unlatch Harry's cage door and get it open. Poor Sherwood had expected an easy meal, but what she got instead was the trouncing of her life.

First Harry bit her paw as soon as she thrust it at him. He bit it every time she tried to get him, and just when she decided she didn't want him after all, he got hold of her and wouldn't let go. Then he dived at her and bit her leg. She took off running and soon outdistanced him.

"I'm building a super hamster," Jack had said proudly after he'd retrieved the biting and kicking Harry and put him back into his cage.

"What you've built," Dad told him, "is a grouchy, cantankerous hamster who wants to get some sleep."

I had thought that when Jack and I went to Aunt Irene's, Harry would have an excellent chance to sleep and—eventually—rest in peace.

"I couldn't do it," Jack said as he tried to calm the hamster down.

"Dad says he won't live much longer anyway."

"We'll see."

"Rodents never live more than a couple years, and they *don't* necessarily hibernate before they die. That article you read must have been talking about sick hamsters."

Jack turned to say something back, and Harry seized his chance. He bit Jack ferociously on the hand and scrambled to the floor. We both dived to grab him and clunked our heads together so hard that we saw stars.

As soon as my head cleared, I saw that Jack had leaned forward, bent down, and put his head between his knees. I was still rubbing my head.

"Do you feel faint?" I asked him.

His voice floated up from between his knees. "No, you mug, I'm looking for him."

"He's probably found a place to hibernate."

"Oh no," he moaned.

"Jack, if Harry doesn't mind, why should you? He's just a hamster. Now sit up."

Suddenly a lady two seats behind us jumped up and screamed. "I've been bitten! Eeeee! A rat! A rat! There's a rat on the train!"

Jack lifted his eyes a little and looked up at me. "I think I'll stay here, thank you."

"Oh, she's right!" A man further down the train yelled. "Stand back! Stand back!" I heard him jump back and begin stomping around.

"Oh," Jack moaned, closing his eyes. "Poor Harry."

"I missed!" the man exclaimed. "It got away." We both sighed with relief. "Someone get the conductor," the man ordered. We both stiffened. I leaned forward and put my head on my knees. "I think I'll join you," I told him.

"If we told them that we're the heroes who broke up the smuggling ring in Peabody, would they go easy on us?" he asked.

"They probably wouldn't even believe us."

We heard the conductor go rushing past. Jack poked his head into the aisle.

"What's he doing?" I asked.

"I dunno. Looking under the seat. Now everybody's looking under the seats."

"Do you see Harry?"

"Uh-uh."

"Here's a hole!" the conductor exclaimed. "He must have run in here. I'll stop it up."

Jack breathed a sigh of relief. "Well, Harry's safe, anyway. He's probably nowhere near that hole. If he'll just behave, everybody will forget about him."

"He's probably asleep by now," I said.

Jack sighed. He sat up straight, and I did, too.

"Hey, mister," he whispered as the conductor went by again, but the conductor didn't notice us. The next time the conductor went by, we both called to him, and he recognized us right away. He was from just outside of Peabody, and he had read about the smugglers and how they'd used the trains. We told him about Harry, and at first he looked a little horrified, but then at last he laughed it off while we were apologizing.

"Poor thing's probably sleeping somewhere," he said. "I'll check that hole later on—after most of the passengers are gone."

He did check it, too, but he never did find Harry. It remained a mystery to us just where the little guy had gone, but I had no doubts that he had found a comfortable sleeping place and had finally gone to sleep.

Jack had brought a portable checkerboard with magnetic pieces, and after the excitement was over, we played checkers for a while. Then we read our books. Then we just sat there, bored and stiff, watching the hills roll by and the telephone lines swoop up and down as we streaked past. A couple times the conductor came by to ask how we were doing, and at noon he told us how to get to the snack car. We bought thick turkey sandwiches and two cans of cola.

On the way back, balancing my sandwich and cola in the swaying car, I noticed this boy who seemed to be sleeping. At first I just glanced at him, but then when I realized how full of holes and ragged his clothes were, I looked at him again. And this time—just for an instant—I thought he was peeking at me under his eyelids. But either I was wrong, or he closed his eyes again.

"Come on, Penny," Jack said from beside me.

We felt better after eating. "Maybe," Jack said, yawning and pushing his seat back as far as it would go so that he could lie down. "Maybe good old Aunt Irene ain't as bad as she's cracked up to be."

I was about to answer, but just then the train let out such a long, low blast of its horn that anything I could have said would have been anticlimactic.

FOURTEEN

A NEW ADVENTURE

The train had been slowing down forever, it seemed. It kept feeling to me like any minute the brakes would be screeching and we would be sliding into the station. The car was dark. Most of the people, including Jack, were asleep or dozing. I couldn't see anything outside in the pitch black night—no friendly house lights, no cars nearby, no gleam of metal or chromium in the night to signal machinery or the siding on a building. Nothing but darkness. Dad had said that Aunt Irene lived in a lonely part of Pennsylvania, down in the south-central part above West Virginia and Maryland. But I had never seen such loneliness as this, and the idea of being sent away to spend the summer was changing in my mind to the thought of being exiled and trapped far from home. I wanted Jack to wake up.

"We're almost there," I said in his ear. "Wake up."

"We're not almost there," he mumbled.

"We are, too."

"Are not."

"Are too, are too."

He opened his brown eyes. "If Aunt Irene doesn't paddle you first thing off this train, I will," he growled.

"Are you scared?" I asked.

"Never! Boys aren't afraid of anything. 'We have nothing to fear, but fear itself!'" he quoted. "And Aunt Irene."

"And Aunt Irene," I agreed.

He nodded and closed his eyes. "For myself, I prefer to hide in my dreams. Maybe you would like to try it, too."

"Jack, we're almost there. The train's slowing down. We have to be awake enough to talk to her."

"The train," he said with a yawn, "has been slowing down for the last half hour. It must have a flat tire."

"I don't think trains have tires."

"Ask the conductor," he said, yawning. He was about to go to sleep again, but the low, wailing horn sounded again, and the train jolted suddenly, slowed down some more, jolted again, and suddenly there were lights outside on one side of the cars—bare electric bulbs strung from the roof of a wooden platform.

The train screeched to a stop. My heart began to beat hard as we silently gathered up our overnight cases. The rest of our luggage was in the baggage car. I glanced at my watch—12:30.

Stiff-legged, stretching their arms, and rubbing their eyes, the dozen or more people in the car were assembling in the aisle, gradually working their way to the door. We fell in line, moving slowly with the crowd down the two steps and then onto the platform outside. A cool breeze stirred through the people. Jack revived some. He stepped ahead of me to get a look at the place.

Then several things happened at once. Something big and black knocked me aside and seemed to hump itself over Jack, and a hoarse man's voice yelled, "Not here, you fool! Take him quietly!"

I screamed without thinking, and then another huge hand pushed me out of its way, and I landed on the wood slats of the platform. I looked up in time to see an enormous walking cane whistle through the air and smack against the shoulders of the bearlike man who was holding Jack by the arm. And then a lady's voice bleated, "Drop him, I say! Drop him, you cutthroat!" Another man was running up, the one who had shouted "Not here."

At first he was going to help his friend, but the older lady was laying about so well with her stick, knocking people right and left, that after a second he thought better of it and shouted, "It's not him! It's not him!"

"It's not him, you—you ruffians!" she squawked. "Drop him! Drop him!" The bearlike man dropped Jack soon enough and tried to get away, butting through the people with his hands over his head, but the lady was going after him pell-mell. They ducked through the people, and those that didn't move fast enough soon wished they had.

I grabbed Jack. "I dropped my wallet" was the first thing he gasped. He had been pulling out his money to tip the baggage man. I saw it and stopped to pick it up before any of the people, now gawking and watching the lady drive the man right off the platform, could trample it. Some of the dollars had shaken loose. I pulled them into my other hand and closed the wallet, but as I straightened up my eyes caught the expression of that ragged boy. He was standing at the back edge of

the platform. He had seen the wallet but hadn't moved toward it, yet he was eyeing the three one-dollar bills in my hand with so much wishfulness that he didn't see me staring at him. Then he did and looked away. He hunched down to edge away.

"Wait!" I called, and my voice came out in a hoarse whisper. Jack was straining to see what had happened to the lady. He didn't see me. The boy turned back. I held out my hand. "Take this!" I said, reaching the dollar bills over the shoulders of the people who were pressing around me and Jack.

He ducked his head, perhaps in thanks, or maybe just in surprise, grabbed the money, and ran to the other side of the platform. He jumped off, bounded across the tracks in front of the waiting train, and disappeared in the shrubs and trees across from the station.

I turned and thrust Jack's wallet into his pocket, whispering, "I owe you three dollars. Are you all right?"

For once he didn't notice what I said about his money. He just nodded. "I'm okay. That guy knocked the wind out of me—Penny, that lady—"

But she was already coming back, pushing her way through the people. She was taller than most of them, ramrod straight with ice-blue eyes and a hard, set mouth. Jack took my hand in one of his.

"Jack and Penny Derwood?" she asked us sternly. "I knew there'd be trouble if both of you came. But nothing takes me by surprise. I'm Aunt Irene."

I said, "How do you do?"

But Jack forgot himself and said, "I just knew it!" Then he realized what he'd said and kind of hunched down as though he thought she might take a crack at him like she'd done to that man.

She only said, "Your bags are coming."

"Who was that man, Aunt Irene?" Jack ventured. "Who did he think I was?"

"A hooligan!" she snapped. "A hooligan! Where is that baggage? Stay here!" And she stamped away.

"Does she mean that he was a hooligan, or that he thought I was a hooligan?" Jack asked me. "Or was she just calling me a hooligan?"

"I don't know."

"What *is* a hooligan?"

"It's a kind of Irishman, I think."

She stamped back with the apologetic baggage man behind her. "Well, let's go," she said, and I noticed that nobody on the platform dared interfere with her.

We fell into step behind her, and she led us off the platform and down a gravelly road to a dusty green station wagon. The baggage man loaded it up, and Jack and I both climbed into the middle seats. Neither of us wanted to sit next to her.

We pulled out and drove in silence down a highway and then onto a winding road. "I suppose the trip was long and dirty?" she asked at last.

"Yes ma'am," I said, too scared to disagree.

"Awfully dirty," Jack added helpfully.

"And your mother, she's probably uncomfortable and not looked after nearly as she ought to be," she continued.

"Not nearly," I said faintly.

"As I thought," she barked. "As I thought. What business did that dog have knocking her down in the snow? What business? What nincompoop was in charge of that dog, anyway? Why was he running around in *your* yard? What nincompoop, *nincompoop,* I say, was in charge of that dog?"

"I was the nincompoop," Jack said softly and repentantly.

"Well, how are you then?" she asked. "Did that hooligan hurt you?"

"I don't think so—bruised my arm, maybe."

She said no more after that, and we rode along in dreadful silence. For once, Jack was more miserable than I was. Up until then nobody had blamed Jack for Mom's accident, and, as frightened as I was of Aunt Irene, I felt some anger. Jack hadn't meant to hurt anybody.

The car was driving through a narrow tunnel under the trees. This, I told myself, is where Hansel and Gretel meet the twentieth century, being chauffeured to their doom in a station wagon. I pressed Jack's hand, still clasped in mine. And then I remembered the boy on the platform, with his ragged jacket and pants that were too short for his legs. Why had I given him the money? Would Jack be mad?

At first I told myself it was really a stupid thing to do, because now I owed Jack three dollars. But then I remembered how the boy's wide blue eyes had looked so startled and so grateful. He had seemed so wishful— so hungry. That was it, hungry. The skin under his red freckles had been goose white. Yes. I straightened in my seat at the memory. Suddenly I knew what people meant when they said that somebody's face looked thin. The boy's cheekbones had stood out, his eyes, though wide with surprise and gratitude, had been sunken— not just hungry, but starving. That was the word. Aunt Irene was looking at me in the rearview mirror. I relaxed and sank back into the seat. But I pressed Jack's hand more confidently. Somewhere out in the dark night we had made a friend, somebody who knew we would be kind to him, and suddenly the summer didn't seem so lonely. Somebody was in worse shape than we were, and I felt sure that if he could find us, he would return.

I would tell Jack later, explain what I had done with his three dollars. It would cheer him up to think about somebody to make friends with.

At last the car's headlights swept across the front of an old farmhouse. This was where my mother had lived with her eleven brothers and sisters, raised mostly by Aunt Irene, the oldest sister. Aunt Irene parked the car.

"You can get your baggage while I unlock," she said. We obeyed her. It was already impossible to disobey her; Aunt Irene, I was sure, would know everything I did, and she seemed pretty handy with punishment. Jack and I lugged the suitcases up the gravel driveway and into a paneled living room.

It smelled like wood—old, clean, polished wood. The light from the lamps, fashioned after hurricane lamps, gleamed off sturdy bentwood rocking chairs with wicker backs and seats. A stone fireplace, built from uncut rock, took up almost one whole wall. Kerosene lamps stood on the mantle. The fire screen was trimmed with brass, and a gleaming brass eagle hung on one wall. There were several paintings of farmlands and one of a dry, dirt road with two narrow wheel ruts that led off around a bend, followed by a falling barbed-wire fence. I looked down at the wide throw rugs that covered the hardwood floor. My mother had told me that they had been poor, but this house was beautiful.

"Hasn't always looked like this," Aunt Irene said gruffly, when she saw my face. "Your mother's told you about the hard times, I have no doubt."

"She has," I replied. We set our bags down.

Aunt Irene cleared her throat. "Now listen, you two," she said sternly. "I've heard about you—heard about your cutting capers all the time. Well, I'm nobody's fool, do you understand? Nobody's fool. You do what I say, when I say it, and no backtalk, and none of your pranks. Do you understand?"

We both nodded. Her words fell on us like the cuts of a whip, and the cozy living room lost all of its welcome.

"I've never had kids—that you know—but I've raised eleven of 'em. Eleven of 'em, mind you, when I wasn't much older than you, girl. So you mind me, do you understand? Do you now?"

"Y-yes," I stammered, and my knees were trembling. Jack said nothing, only ducked his head. Poor Jack! He could make friends with two policemen who thought he'd been throwing rocks at store windows, and he had won over the Ladies' Auxiliary Missionary Fellowship, but he couldn't do anything about the distrust of Aunt Irene.

"Now I know you're tired. Penny, your room is at the top of the front stairs, and Jack, yours is up by the back steps above the kitchen. Go quick now, and get your things put away and your pajamas on."

So we lugged our stuff upstairs while she went into the kitchen, and Jack was silent the whole time. He went down the long, narrow hallway to his room, while I went into mine.

There was a single bed covered with a rough kind of bedspread done in wide black and red squares, like a big checkerboard, and a tall chest of drawers that also smelled fresh and clean and woody. A small desk stood in one corner, and I saw that there were already some papers in it. I didn't have a chance to search through it much, but I thought the desk would make a nice place to write letters home and read books. One lamp—made to look like a hurricane lamp—was fastened to the wall, and another lamp stood on a small stand by the bed.

Somebody had nailed a net up in one corner, and it hung from the wall, stuck in places with seashells. A map, stiff and yellowed with age, hung on the wall alongside it. At first I thought it must be a map of the sea to go along with the net and the shells, but when I looked at it I saw that it was more like a mosaic than a map, and it was of the woods in the area, with drawings here and there to represent houses.

I unpacked my clothes, put them away in the tall chest, and then slipped into my pajamas and robe. I tiptoed out into the hall. Jack was coming.

"We have to pray," he whispered to me. I nodded at the hallway floor.

"Let's do it right here," I said. "Aunt Irene's down in the kitchen."

We felt too awkward and scared to kneel, so we sat. Jack went first, whispering his prayers with a voice that shook sometimes. I found it hard to concentrate that first time on what he was saying—he sounded so afraid and nervous, so unlike Jack. We hadn't talked about it, but by silent agreement we prayed only for Mom and the others—it seemed rude to Aunt Irene to admit to each other how miserable we felt.

Then it was my turn, and I prayed for Mom first and went all the way down the line: Dad, Jean, Renee, Freddy, and Marie. It didn't take me more than a minute or two, feeling so awkward as I was, and then I looked up at Jack, wanting to make him feel better. But he was looking over my shoulder. I turned around, and there was Aunt Irene, standing right behind me.

"I've made hot chocolate downstairs," she said. "It gets cool here at night, and you'll want something warm before you go to bed."

FIFTEEN

NEW FRIENDS—
MR. LAMERSON
AND HUMPHREY

The next morning our breakfast was silent. Aunt Irene fixed oatmeal and bacon and muffins and coffee and orange juice. But it was so dead quiet and we were so homesick, we could barely eat. I was resolute, determined to force it down, hoping Aunt Irene wouldn't notice how Jack was just poking his spoon around in his bowl. I didn't want him to get in trouble.

At last she said, "There now, I've cooked too much. I'm not used to cooking for more than one or less than a dozen." It was the first joke she had made. "If you two have had enough, you may leave the table."

Dad had told us that we absolutely had to do the dishes for Aunt Irene at every meal, so we just stood up and started clearing the table without saying anything.

"Here now, what's this?" she asked us.

"My father said—" I began quietly.

"Oh! Yes, told you to be helpful." She didn't seem to know what to say; then she let out a harumph and tried a smile but didn't quite manage one. "Well then, Jack, you go up and make the beds while your sister helps me down here." Her words sent a stab of dread to my heart. Alone in the silence with Aunt Irene! Jack ducked his head and went upstairs. I gathered the plates up and took them to the sink.

After I cleared the table with her, I turned on the hot water and found the bottle of liquid soap in the cabinet under the sink. Just as I straightened up, her hand touched the back of my neck.

"You and your brother are welcome in my house, Penny," she said. Her slate-blue eyes were still as keen as ever, but her mouth wasn't as firmly set. "Sometimes I handle my words badly, and I see I hurt you with them last night, but you are welcome here. I haven't ever in my life sent anybody away hungry or in want, and I wouldn't turn away my own niece and nephew." Then she looked away and harumphed loudly, clattered through the silverware, and furiously started drying the dishes. I wondered if she realized that we weren't really her niece and nephew—not by blood ties, anyway.

After the morning chores were done, she sent us out to play, and for the first time since last night we really relaxed. Aunt Irene told us not to go any farther than the creek that was within sight of the house, so we went down and looked at it. The water was low, just past my ankles. We looked for turtles and salamanders. Jack found a black snake and caught him. I wouldn't let him bring it near me, but he was in love with it, even after it bit him with its needlelike teeth.

"What if he's poisonous?" I asked.

"Oh, he's not poisonous! Look at that innocent face!" And he held up the snake's spade-shaped face for me to look at. The snake flipped its tongue out and vibrated it at me. "I'll name him Humphrey," Jack said.

Jack was sure he could tame it, so he played with it for a while. Then we climbed onto an enormous tree root that was thrust out from the steep bank. We sat on the root and talked.

Jack looked better. The morning sunlight shone on his auburn hair, and he was smiling, but he still seemed a little homesick. I told him about the three dollars I had taken and given to the boy on the train platform.

"Just pay me back half of it," he told me. "I'd like to think I helped him, too. I wonder who he was. What did he look like?"

"He was about your size, about your age. He had blue eyes and bright red hair, and he wore a knit cap," I said. "That's about all that I can remember. He looked hungry and sick."

"What was he wearing?" Jack asked.

"I'm not sure. It was pretty sloppy. The jacket was a blue sweatshirt jacket with holes in it, like he'd gotten it out of a trash can somewhere. I didn't notice the rest. There was something in his face—like he was scared— I don't know how to say it. I felt sorry for him as soon as I saw him."

Jack sighed and readjusted himself on the limb. "Maybe those men were after him," he said at last. "They were kidnapers, maybe, looking for him for some reason. Only, they got me by accident."

"You don't look alike."

"You said we were the same size," he pointed out.

"His hair is flaming red."

Jack ran his fingers through his short auburn hair. "What if those guys were working for somebody else, Penny? And all they knew was that they had to find a kid that was my size, my age, with reddish hair? If they'd never seen a picture of the kid, they might jump to conclusions, especially if I walked off the very train they were expecting him to be on. My hair is at least reddish, and I was wearing a blue jacket, too, even though mine is a windbreaker."

I dangled my feet over the water. "What would those two guys want with a kid?" I asked. "He can't be more than eleven years old. For a minute last night I thought those guys were from Tom Thumb's gang, coming to kidnap us, but I guess not."

Jack didn't say anything. He still felt mighty serious.

"Did Aunt Irene say anything to you today?" I asked.

"She told me to make myself at home—within reason," he said. He laughed. "First I get paddled for stealing a mattress, then two policemen think I'm a crook, then two thugs try to kidnap me, then Aunt Irene tells me not to try anything while I'm here. I knew I had a dishonest face." He stopped and then looked at me. In spite of his jokes, he was still sad.

"You know, Jack, if we could find that kid again, things might seem better," I said. "We could at least make a friend."

Suddenly Jack's eyes locked on something, and he froze. "There he is!" he whispered. "No, don't jump, or he'll run. Act like you're not looking for him. Keep your eyes down!" He forced himself to act normal again, swinging his legs over the muddy water.

I studiously examined the wood surface of the limb. "If you're teasing me, Jack—"

"He's got red hair all right, and a gray flannel shirt under the blue jacket," Jack said quietly.

"Yes, that's right. Now I remember," I said. "His shirt was a gray flannel. Is he coming closer?"

"No, he's just watching us. He must know I've spotted him. Man, it's a good thing I'm such a cheapskate," Jack said.

"Why?" I asked.

"Because I've got money to spend—my own money." He reached into his back pocket and pulled out his wallet. He took out a couple of dollars and stuffed them down into a wedge in the wood. "I'm going to walk back to the house, then you come, too," he said. "Don't look back at him, or he'll run away for sure. See you in a minute." He stood up and stretched, balancing easily on the root, and then strode back to the bank, stepped up onto the grass, and walked toward the big house, whistling and stopping every now and then to toss a rock across the waving meadow. After a minute or two I followed him. I never looked back, and I acted as indifferent as Jack did, because I wondered the same thing he was wondering. If our red-haired friend were watching us, maybe those two thugs were watching us too, or maybe they were out looking for him. But behind me, down in the creek bed, I was sure I heard the creak of the enormous root as somebody cautiously stepped onto it, carefully balancing and stepping out on it to get the money. So he had seen Jack put it there for him.

* * * * * *

"Aunt Irene," Jack said at lunch as we ate in the dining room.

"Yes?" she tried not to rumble at him or eye him too keenly. I could see she was trying not to keep us so scared, but she seemed like a frightening sort of person, and it was hard for her.

"Who were those two men at the station last night?"

The keen eyes lighted up at the memory of the battle. "Hooligans!" she snapped. "Or . . . truant officers!"

"But Jack's not a truant," I said.

"There was another boy who got off the train just before you—sure looked like a runaway. I wouldn't be surprised if those two lunkheads saw Jack first and figured he was the other boy. How's your arm?" she asked him.

Jack rolled up his sleeve and proudly displayed a bruise on his right arm. "That's where he grabbed me on that arm. It hurt all right."

"They played a little rough, but I played somewhat rougher!" Her eyes blazed proudly. "That's what they were, truant officers, I'm sure. Well, next time they'll learn to ask before they tackle so roughly." Then she subsided into snorting to herself in disgust and muttering about what the world was coming to, and who *could* you trust when a juvenile officer would tackle an eleven-year-old boy.

All in all, she seemed a little easier to talk to today, even though she muttered to herself and looked fierce at the memory of the tussle at the train station. I could see Jack working himself up to being friendly. He put his hand on her lean wrist and said, "Thank you, Aunt Irene, for chasing away those—"

But suddenly she slid her chair back and jumped up. "Lands! There he is again! Where's that stick?"

Our eyes went to the window, and we were half-expecting to see the red-haired boy again.

"That varmint! What's it take to teach him? There it is!" She picked up the cane from a corner and flew outside with it. We ran to the window. There was a dog out there, a magnificent collie—brown and white and gold—with a broad, frilly chest and long, fawn-colored muzzle.

"Oh!" we both exclaimed together. He was so beautiful, standing poised on the smooth, green grass.

Aunt Irene, brandishing her cane, went leaping down the porch steps. "Scat! Scat! Out of my rosebushes, you mongrel! Go on, git!"

He barked joyously at sight of her and ran toward her.

"Git, I say! Git! Take that! Take that! Hold still a minute, will you!" She was hitting everywhere with the cane, but the dog, barking triumphantly, leaped from side to side, back and then in again, tail wagging, head ducking up and down, avoiding the slashes of the cane as though he were jumping rope with it. He grabbed the hem of her dress and tugged. "Down I say! Mad dog! Mad dog!" and she aimed a terrific blow at him, but he sidestepped it like a flash and then grabbed her hem again and pulled. "Aagh! Let go, I say! Let go! Scat! Scat!"

This complicated dance between the two of them went on for another minute, until, from sheer joy the dog ran a circle around her and then loped off, stopping every now and then to bark at her and invite her to chase him into the woods, but she let him go.

Jack and I scurried back to the table and slid into our chairs. In another moment she stamped inside, set the cane in its corner, and took her chair again. We kept our heads down, but I could feel her eyes on us. At last I heard her pick up her fork, and she started muttering to herself about flea-bitten varmints and leash laws.

After lunch she said, "Here now, I'll wash the dishes. You two better get to know the lay of the land. Go on out and follow this road. It curves right around the foot of Granny's Mountain there." She pointed at the big wooded hill that rose just beyond the creek. "Keep to the road, and you'll come to town. It's about two miles. Pick me up a loaf of bread, will you?"

We nodded, and she went to get her purse. She came back and handed the money to me. "You may want a rest and a cold drink before you start back. Sam Lamerson's got a soft-drink cooler there at the grocery store."

I thanked her, but she only harumphed and went into the kitchen.

"This is great!" Jack whispered.

"You call walking two miles great?" I asked.

"The storekeeper," he said. "The storekeeper, don't you see?"

"No. What are you talking about?"

"Come on. I'll tell you while we walk. And maybe that dog will find us, too." He grinned, tossed a quarter up, caught it, and said, "Maybe it's not going to be such a bad summer after all."

As soon as we were on our way and the house was almost out of sight behind us, I said, "What about the storekeeper?"

"It's simple," he told me. "Twice now we've left money for that kid, right?"

"Right."

"So he's got to be using it. The storekeeper will be able to tell us about him. If the kid has come in and bought food from him, then we know the kid's a runaway like Aunt Irene said, but if the kid's been buying—say, uranium—then we know that this is no mere runaway. He's a horse of a different feather, so to speak."

"That's horse of a different *color*," I told him. "And I doubt that the kid is buying uranium from the grocery store."

He nodded. "It was a long shot; I'll admit that. Still, you never know what these little out-of-the-way grocery stores keep in stock."

"And what happens if we meet those two thugs?" I asked.

He grinned. "*Amy Belle and the Moon Surface Oil Rig Caper,* page 38! It's worked before. But those guys really were rough. I hope we don't meet them a second time."

"Not without Aunt Irene," I added.

He laughed. "She held them at bay pretty well, didn't she? She's all gray and wrinkled looking, but she packs a wallop. I've never seen a stronger woman."

"Are you afraid of her?" I asked.

He nodded. "Just when I think she might really be nice, she goes chasing after dogs, trying to knock their brains out."

"The dog wasn't scared."

"No, but he *was* fast." Jack rolled his eyes. "I'm not that fast."

We walked on in silence. The road was dusty, and shrubbery grew densely along it. The trees thinned out, giving way to fields overgrown with brush. In all directions the horizon was crowded with smoky blue mountains that looked soft and alive in the haze. We came to a paved road and turned left; in another few minutes we rounded a bend, and there was the town— a gas station, a small grocery store, several beautiful white houses, and some storefront businesses. A few narrow roads turned off the main street, but I don't think they really led anywhere. They just made room for a few more houses and storefronts.

A few old pickup trucks were parked along the street, the kind of pickups with rounded fenders and headlights, like you might see in an encyclopedia article on the history of motor vehicles. Part of the sidewalk was made from boards and part was of concrete.

"Keep your eyes peeled for gangsters," Jack said out of the side of his mouth. "If you see any, then we'll know we really just stepped back in time."

We found the grocery store without difficulty. It was cooler inside, but I noticed it wasn't air-conditioned. It smelled like a butcher shop. A middle-aged man behind the only cash register nodded at us. "You're new in town, eh?"

I nodded, and Jack said, "We're staying with our aunt."

"Oh, I see. Your Aunt Irene, I expect. Yep, I heard she was having kids come up for the summer. She's quite a lady, that Irene, quite a lady." And, having made that obvious comment, he beamed at us.

It was nice having somebody speak so kindly to us. We got the bread, and as we were paying for it, Jack said, "Do you know my aunt well, sir?"

"Middling well, only middling. I'm an elder at the church, you know, and there's none more faithful than your Aunt Irene, no sir! But I expect she takes some getting used to, doesn't she? Well, that's all right. That grainy covering hides a tender inside, I'll tell you."

Jack and I glanced at each other. "Oh, go on now," the storekeeper laughed at us. "You're too young to be cynics!"

"What's a cynic?" Jack whispered.

But I kicked him and asked, "We'd like to buy two sodas. Do you have any cold bottles?"

"Yep, back there. Take your pick."

We went and picked out two bottles—cola for me and grape for Jack.

"Soda!" the man laughed, ringing it up. "We call it pop here. Well now, where was I? Oh, your Aunt Irene. Well now, she got quite a crust on her from raising her own brothers and sisters, she did, but times were bad then, pretty bad. And I reckon half the time she wasn't sure what she was about, but she had to pretend she was sure. This town's pretty peaceful now, but in those days we had the bootleggers coming through and building their stills, and your aunt was just determined to fight 'em. Yes she was!"

"What's a bootlegger?" Jack asked.

The storekeeper laughed and slapped the counter. "Now I know I've lived too long! Son, are you really that wet behind the ears?"

Jack automatically touched his ear and glanced at me, puzzled.

"Well, come on then," the man said. "There's crates out by the door, and business is slow on these hot afternoons. I can see your education hasn't been complete. I got a story or two that you'll like, and maybe you'll see what a fine gal your aunt is for what she done. Yes, indeed. And I'll tell you something else: the little young 'uns are scared of her, and the folks that know better say she's eccentric, but those of us who grew up with her wouldn't trade her for nothing—not nothing!"

SIXTEEN

THE STOREKEEPER'S STORY

Jack and Sam Lamerson and I went out onto the sidewalk and sat on crates in the shade cast by the store itself. The storekeeper reached down to pick a few round cockleburs off the cuffs of his pants. He flicked them into the street and glanced at his watch. "Don't let me run on too long, now," he said, and told us his story.

"You may not know what Prohibition was—a decade or so between the two world wars when alcoholic drinks were illegal.

"For myself I think that most people were glad to have the country be rid of such a torment as alcohol. But there were some of course—and a good deal of these were very rich—who wanted their whiskey and were determined to get it. So men out in the country, especially country like this, where there's plenty of valleys and lots of shrub and brush, set up their own distilling vats, or *stills*, as we call them.

"These men would brew their whiskey and then carry it over state lines into West Virginia and Maryland. They were called bootleggers because plenty of times they'd

slip the narrow whiskey flasks down into their boots to hide what they were doing.

"Now I'll tell you, it was a bad business. There were gangsters mixed up in it, especially in transporting the whiskey across state lines, and families were ruined from it, and men were killed, either from the whiskey itself or from battling with the police or other bootleggers.

"At first, you see, everybody in these parts hated the bootlegging business. Like I said, anybody with a family and kids wanted them to be kept safe. But then along came the idea that drinking that stuff was glamorous, and since rich people did it, why shouldn't anybody else? See, it used to be that you thought of a bootlegger as a smelly old rascal dressed in rags and lying in a stupor all day. But then the Hollywood movie business was going great guns, and they started playing up that maybe wine and whiskey had its lighter side. You know, a person could be all dressed up and have a drink of it, and it wouldn't hurt him.

"Then people began to think maybe it wouldn't do to have the United States government outlaw liquor. They thought maybe the laws were too tough. And then we had the Great Depression—that was when lots of folks were out of work and hungry—and some people figured maybe if alcohol were legal there'd be jobs for people. So the government ended Prohibition. But up here, being so close to the Virginia and Maryland state lines, the bootleggers went right on working. You see, they already had their own customers and their own rates, and they didn't aim to lose their businesses. They could sell it cheaper than the liquor stores, and without any tax on it.

"And these bootleggers were slick and smart. The others had all been weeded out by now, but these boys knew how to make friends, and don't think they ignored people in need—no sirree! They'd come riding right into this town with a couple hundred dollars for some poor family they'd heard about where the man wasn't working and the kids were down sick. And they'd make a big show of helping them out. Oh yes, they were slick all right. These boys knew how to say 'yes sir' and 'yes ma'am' and take an older woman's arm to help her across the street and everything else that any Boy Scout handbook would teach 'em to do. Pretty soon the people around here weren't so hard on them anymore. So long as the bootleggers were good to us, we left 'em in peace. We knew that they were up there in the hills brewing that poison. But we left 'em be, to our shame.

"Then one day one of 'em—Will Birky—he came down all slicked out and driving a flashy automobile— yes, a real automobile! I tell you, we hadn't seen many of them up here in this little town. I was just toddling then, but I remember seeing the car all right, and feeling like something magnificent and grand had happened to all of us.

"Well, Birky had seen this real pretty gal, Irene Holmes, coming home from church one day, and he wanted to court her. At first she said no right off. She didn't want to marry any dirty old bootlegger. But she was a poor girl and had done without all of her life, and times were getting harder.

"He just kept it up, wooing her and trying to help her as much as he could and even coming to church and acting all pious and nice and reverent. She finally let him speak with her more freely, and pretty soon it was known that they were courting. My father was the pastor then, and he warned her—pleaded with her not to throw her life away for a sweet-talkin' bootlegger like Birky.

"But at last Birky proposed, and they married, eloped, I believe, and came back here and settled down. They seemed happy for a while. He looked to have given up his bootlegging—that's what folks thought. After a year they had their first little girl—that's your Aunt Irene, by the way—and then a year later they had a son. The family got bigger, and money was coming up scarcer, so finally Birky went back to his still up in the mountains, and I reckon he did a good business, because no one was slicker than him.

"Folks in town got a little upset because they knew what he was doing, and they didn't want a bootlegger living so elegant so close to the town. His wife, she'd given up church after they'd gotten married, but with him gone so much, she wanted to go back to it. He found out and got mad, wouldn't let her go, and wouldn't let her teach their children the Bible. He said he was going to teach his sons *his* trade so they'd never have to come kneeling and weeping to any stuck-up preacher.

"Your poor grandmother's heart broke because she knew then what she'd done, and your Aunt Irene was growing up, and she came to see how unhappy her mother was.

"Well, your Grandfather Birky, he just got fiercer as time went by. He drank more and sold less—at least, he brought less and less home—and then he came home less and less from the hills. Finally he never did come back, even though some men from the town went out riding to look for him up there and nearly got their hats shot off.

"Your grandmother was still a young thing, scarce past thirty, and she did come back to the church, repentant over what she'd done to herself and her children and the Lord's name. She was broken-hearted, poor girl, and died a couple of years after that, just when her oldest daughter Irene had turned sixteen. So that's how your Aunt Irene came to take care of her whole family on her own.

"And, oh my, the times she had! For her father had made friends up in those hills, and every now and then they'd come down to borrow money or to find a hide-out. Sure enough, they'd go straight to her because they knew her and they knew the house was set out of town a little way. They'd invent some crazy story about a favor that the family owed them and try to scare her into helping them.

"Well, Irene was terrified of her brothers becoming bootleggers, and she knew perfectly well that these men might just try to win a few of them over. So no matter what these men said or threatened, she stood firm. No money, no help, nothin'.

"One time she came into the house from the garden and there were your Aunts Mabel and Gertrude, both of them under twelve years old, waiting on two bootleggers, filling them up with sausage and eggs. And one of those rascals was holding the youngest—Molly. Your Aunt Irene never said nothing, just took down the old shotgun off the wall and started counting down from five. Didn't those fellows jump then! They moved so fast they nearly left their shadows behind.

"And then one time when your Uncle Justin was just thirteen, one of those scoundrels cornered him in the shed and told Justin he was going to take him to his father up in the woods.

" 'My father's dead,' Justin said, because that's what most people supposed. And the bootlegger laughed and said, 'No, Birky isn't dead, either.' He started telling Justin how the bootleggers all lived like kings up there, but Justin was scared and started to cry.

"Well, your Aunt Irene walked into the shed just when the bootlegger was asking Justin if he didn't want to live like a king. She grabbed up a broomstick without any broom on it and cracked that bootlegger over the head with it. 'There's your crown!' she snapped at him, and then she clunked and clunked him and yelled for Justin to run for the sheriff.

"Well, the bootlegger, he tried to get away, but your Aunt Irene was furious, and she knew she'd come through a narrow squeak at almost losing Justin, so she reckoned to make an example of this scoundrel. She parried with him back and forth, as ferocious as she could be, and held him there a good half hour until the sheriff came. And that was one bootlegger who cooled his heels for a while.

"She was fast, was your aunt, and she was scared, too. The family was poor again, and she knew as the boys got older that they might be powerfully tempted to make some big money up in those hills. How she preached at them! As soon as they'd get old enough, she'd have them sworn into the Temperance League before they could blink twice."

The storekeeper leaned back against the window of his store. "That's a good piece of it," he said. "And none of it's a secret. Folks still like to hear those stories of how your aunt went and outwitted all them bootleggers. I'm surprised she hasn't told you herself."

"Well, I knew my aunt had raised my mother and the others," I said. "That youngest one, Molly, that's my mother."

"Mom only told us the funny parts," Jack put in, "the parts that her older brothers and sisters told her, like how Aunt Irene chased that guy around the shed. I guess by the time Mom was old enough to know what was going on, the bootleggers were leaving the family alone."

He nodded. "Yes, Molly was spared most of it, and your Aunt Irene managed to shuttle the younger ones off to relatives a lot to keep them from being hounded at all by the bootleggers. But see here, you don't have cause to be afraid of your Aunt Irene. She's a crusty girl and strong as a team of mules, but she's true as steel, and if she ever was scared of anything, she's never let on to it."

"Are there still bootleggers up there?" I asked.

He smiled. "Oh, no. Not in these parts any more. The forestry people came in with their conservation programs and chased a lot of them out by accident. And of course the old gang of them broke up by and by as each member got older or went to jail." He turned his eyes to the mountains that we could see over the rooftops across the street. "Every now and then I guess somebody finds a still up there that's being used, but it's rare."

Just then a dog barked, hailing us. "There's my boy! Here, Tige!"

"That's the collie!" Jack exclaimed. "Is he yours?"

"No, more's the pity. I could never afford a dog like Tige." Tige came up, sniffed at us politely, then blissfully buried his muzzle into the storekeeper's cupped hand.

"He likes you," Jack said.

"Yes, we're friends from way back. There are some estates further down from your aunt's house. Somebody down there probably owns him. They keep him brushed anyway. But he gets his affection from the people around town." Jack and I glanced at each other. It looked like Aunt Irene was giving him something a lot different from affection, but we didn't say anything about it. "Yes sir," he said. "I often take Tige up in the hills with me when I hunt or walk. We sure do love to roam together." And he smiled, the picture of a happy man.

SEVENTEEN

ANOTHER SIDE OF AUNT IRENE

Jack and I finished our drinks. "Say," Jack said at last. "Have you seen a kid around here, a new kid like us, with red hair?" The storekeeper eyed Jack up and down before answering, and Jack, reading the sudden suspicion, continued, "He came in with us on the train, you see. We thought we might make friends with him."

"Didn't he seem a bit odd to you?" the storekeeper asked. So he did know him!

"A little," Jack admitted. "He didn't have much to say for himself."

"Why, that'll be—" but the the storekeeper stopped himself from explaining it. He looked at us. "Hmph," he said at last. "You two are smart and well-meaning, I reckon. But you don't let on to all you know, do you?" Jack and I looked at each other, and then we eyed the storekeeper. It was our turn to be suspicious. Just because the man said he was an elder and told a few good stories didn't make him genuine.

"You're not letting on either," I said pointedly.

"And I'm not going to," he said. "You'd do best to stay away from the boy. Leave him be and don't go looking for him. Now I've told you nothing, you hear me? But I've told you plenty. Don't look for him."

Jack stood up. "Thank you," he said. "We aren't going to let on anything to anybody. And for right now we won't look for him."

"Jack!" I exclaimed. The storekeeper nodded.

"You're good kids. You'd better get on home, now."

As we walked down the quiet main street, I said, "How could you promise such a thing? Not look for him? We've got to look for him!"

"No we don't, Penny. He's already found us, hasn't he? Let's leave it up to him. If he's in trouble or hungry, he'll come to us again. And you can hang your hat on the fact that he's been to the storekeeper back there. That guy knows where he is and what's going on. Come on, let's look around some of these other stores."

We did look around for a while, but there wasn't much to see: a hardware store and a seamstress shop. After about a half hour of roaming, we took to the road again. Jack thrust his hands in his pockets and looked around at the trees and shrubs and the rough terrain. "It's hard to imagine this place full of criminals. It's so peaceful. I wonder what it's like up there where there aren't any houses? There's plenty of trails," he said.

"Maybe Aunt Irene will let us go hiking some day."

He nodded. "I'd like to look at the map in your room. Would you mind?"

"Just be careful with it, Jack. It's old. It may fall apart."

"I'll be careful," he promised.

We walked along without talking for a while, and then Jack said, "Do you hear something? Barking?"

I was about to say no, but then I did hear barking, and in another minute the collie came bursting from the shrubs, all stuck full of twigs and leaves and cockleburs in his beautiful coat. He bounded over to us, barking.

"What a beauty!" Jack exclaimed, kneeling down fearlessly and opening his arms to the dog. The collie bounded up to us, licked at Jack's face, and tried to leap up and lick mine. I knelt down, too, and we petted him. He barked happily and romped around us. "It's too hot!" Jack called to him. "If you want to play, you'll have to get my Aunt Irene to take a few swings at you again."

"Say, I thought the storekeeper said this dog was brushed often," I exclaimed. "He's stuck full of twigs and stuff—cockleburs, too."

"He must have just come back from roaming around. He was clean when we petted him at the store," Jack said.

"I wonder if the storekeeper was out roaming with him," I said, looking up at Jack. He shrugged, and we walked on.

The dog swung off into the bushes, but came out again and tagged along. Every now and then he would leave to follow a scent or explore something, but he kept returning. "I wonder who owns him," Jack said. By this time we were passing the creek bottom, and through the trees we heard a whistle. The dog bounded away.

"Maybe we should go see," I suggested.

"No, we're late enough as it is, and I don't want to have him get too close to the house. Aunt Irene might not like it."

We trudged up to the house. I had the bread, so I went into the kitchen while Jack went upstairs to look at the map on my wall. Aunt Irene was in the kitchen, sitting at the little breakfast table, reading a book while she peeled potatoes. She would read a paragraph or two, furiously peel away an entire potato skin in one long curl, then read some more.

"I thought maybe you'd gotten lost," she said as I came in and put the loaf in the bread box.

"The man who runs the store told us stories," I said.

"Sam Lamerson," she put in. "He's a yarnspinner," she agreed. "He didn't fill your head with ghost stories and that nonsense, did he?"

"No. He told us—" I looked down. "He told us about the bootlegger in the shed and those stories. I had only heard parts of them, and he told us what we'd missed before."

"Why, I could have told you those." She looked up sharply, trying to get a look at my face. At last she said, "I see he told you quite a bit you never heard before. Sit down."

I sat down, and she passed a cutting of potato to me. I'd never tried raw potato, but it wasn't bad. It crunched a lot.

"Times were hard then," she observed. "But then again times are never easy. But even with bootleggers all around us and nobody older than me to tell me what to do, I managed. The Lord brought me through somehow, and I didn't lose a single brother to those bootleggers—that is, except your Uncle Bill, and that was only for a summer. It wasn't three months before his heart was broken and he came home repentant. Said he'd rather starve than have a part in that business."

She stopped and whittled away at a potato. Then she looked up at me. "Your Jack, he's a lot like my Bill— real smart and sensitive. Oh, don't act surprised now. You know the boy is, even though from what I hear he plays the clown more than he should—" and some of her fierceness seemed to return on this, but she suppressed it. "That's how my Bill was—still is. He writes me from California, and he sounds happy-go-lucky as always, him being a lawyer and everything. Harumph! Clowns just run in the family, I suppose, but I never did have much time for laughing at them when I was a girl like you. Go on now, you'd better find your brother."

I stood up, a little surprised at being dismissed so abruptly. "I'll take the back steps," I said quietly. I wanted to walk past her. Yes, her eyes were wet—from thinking about the past, I expect. Without thinking about what she might do, I leaned forward, kissed her cheek, and then darted back as though she might explode from it.

"Go on now!" she exclaimed fiercely. "You're too old for that!"

And I scurried up the steps, not sure if she'd hurt my feelings or if somehow I had hurt hers.

* * * * * *

Dinner was mostly silent except for her questions and our answers. But she seemed more agitated, and even I could see that she wore her harumphing and grumbling like a cloak sometimes. I wasn't as afraid of her as I had been, but I felt more and more like we made her uncomfortable, like we had invaded her happy, grumbling little world. For the second time in two days I wanted to go home. I even forgot about the red-haired boy. I wanted my mother and home and my own church and friends and to have a good fight with Jack like in the old days and have Mom or Dad break it up and make us behave. I felt like I was growing up, and I didn't like it.

Later, after we had done the dishes, Jack and I looked at the map. It had the houses drawn on it in minute detail—beautiful artwork, including some things that looked like cartoons, and here and there were ink drawings of trees labeled in tiny print, like "white birch" or "hemlock" or "palmetto." The houses and the town seemed to have been drawn exactly where they belonged on the map, only blown up out of proportion with the map scale. But the trees were dotted here and there, and I didn't think anybody would have been crazy enough to chart every tree in the forest, nor even clumps of them.

"Maybe it's where the mapmaker had gone to cut wood, and that was what he got in each spot," Jack guessed. "This way he knew where he shouldn't bother to go a second time."

"Maybe," I agreed.

At last we hung the map back on the wall and prayed together. "Dad said he would call us on Saturday," Jack reminded me. "That's tomorrow." That cheered me up a little. He said good-night, and I went into my room. I sat at my desk and thought about Mom and the other kids, and then I looked out the window at the dark night without any cheerful streetlights or houses below, and I felt so lonely and trapped that I wanted to cry. I didn't care if Aunt Irene had chased off bootleggers and gangsters and raised eleven brothers and sisters all by herself. I wanted to go home.

I flipped off the light switch and crawled into bed, curling myself into a miserable little ball scrunched up against the wall. Soon I heard Aunt Irene's footsteps out on the hardwood floor of the hallway, and the door opened a crack.

"Good-night."

"Good-night," I said through gritted teeth. My throat was tight.

But I didn't hear the door close. After a moment it opened wider, letting in a block of dim light from the hallway. Aunt Irene walked over and pulled the chair up by my bed. "I'm sorry," she said. Her hand, strong and warm, rubbed my back through the checkerboard cover. "You took me by surprise this afternoon, and I scolded you right off. Scolding comes natural to me, quicker than thought. Forgive me, Penny. I've given you and Jack a miserable night and a miserable day. I'm not used—" But then she stopped herself. What wasn't she used to, I wondered.

She sat beside me, for a long time saying nothing and only rubbing my back, until finally she asked me very gently, "Are you homesick? I expect you are, especially with your mother being in the hospital. Your father told me that at first they thought it was just a sprain." She went on and on, pausing in case I wanted to answer, then continuing softly when I didn't. "But I know my Molly will be all right, her being so active and all, and healthy. It just takes the doctors time, honey, to sort everything out and prescribe the right treatment. It'll work out. It always does . . ."

And then finally under the warmth on my back and the soft voice all around me, I relaxed and fell asleep. But in my dreams I was standing on the tree root over the creek, staring at the red-haired boy on the opposite bank. And the storekeeper came up behind me. He was holding the map, yelling, "Bootleggers! Bootleggers! Run!"

EIGHTEEN

YET ANOTHER SIDE OF AUNT IRENE

The morning came, gray and rainy, and I dozed in my bed until late, listening to the ticking of the water drops as they struck the window. In the distance, thunder rumbled. It was a rare moment at Aunt Irene's: peaceful.

A blaring squall cut the air, shaking the walls, and I leaped out of bed. Had lightning struck? Was a train coming through? I pushed my thoughts away as I fumbled into my robe, but the thoughts came tumbling back. Had the boiler exploded? Was the house on fire?

WA-ANG-ANG! There it went again. I heard a fierce stumbling up the hall.

"My stars! What's going on?" That was Aunt Irene.

She was rushing by just as I pushed open the door. "It's burglars, bootleggers, Communists! Where's that cane when I need it? Ah!" She took up her trusty weapon and streamed down the hall, gray hair flying, robe trailing behind her. I followed. Somehow, someway, it didn't sound like burglars or bootleggers to me. It sounded more like Jack.

She threw open a door down by Jack's room, just as the same head-splitting, heart-cracking blare came pushing through the joints and walls of the hallway. WA-ANG-ANG!

"My stars! It may be dangerous!" she exclaimed. That probably was meant to keep me back, but I went through the door behind her and found a rickety stairway leading to the attic. As we clumped up, Aunt Irene holding the cane poised for a telling blow, I could hear muttering, "I could make a million dollars with this any day. A million! At least a couple thousand." And then a sharp intake of breath and my aunt and I both put our hands to our ears by instinct.

WA-ANG-ANG!

"My stars!" she exclaimed. My ears were still ringing too much for me to say anything. "My stars!"

We clumped up into the attic. Jack was sitting on somebody's old rocking horse, a navy hat pushed back on his head, and a bugle in his hand. Jack's snake, Humphrey, was coiled around the high, pricked ears of the wooden horse. "Hi!" Jack exclaimed, surprised at the interruption.

"Hi?" Aunt Irene exclaimed. "Hi? What with air-raid sirens a-blowin' at 8:30 in the morning? I'll 'hi' you!" She brandished her cane. "Your poor Aunt Ida—rest her soul! She's turning over in her grave this very moment! And who wouldn't be with that thing a-blowin' to wake the dead? And when I think how beautifully she did blow that thing! My stars, what are you doing, boy?"

"Blowing this bugle," Jack said innocently.

"Lands, I know that! You're a-blowin' it like it's an inner tube!" she exclaimed.

"Watch!" he said, holding it up and taking a short, quick breath.

"No!" Aunt Irene cried in horror, and instantly thrust her cane between the horn and his mouth. He got a mouth full of wood. "Ugh!" He spit out some dust.

"We've heard you three or four times now!" she exclaimed. "I thought the troops were a-pouring in, right through the roof! Your poor Aunt Ida, why she played that thing for Sunday school and at camp meetings, and there you are blaring away. What would she say now? You sound worse than an air horn, boy!"

Jack wasn't hurt. "Can I practice on it?"

"You're a-murdering that poor bugle!" she exclaimed. I wondered if she was mad. But as he started to put it down, she said, "Oh, go 'long and blow on it, if your head's thick enough to stand it. Only blow it outdoors."

"Thanks, Aunt."

"But see here, lemme show you something." She reached over and took it. "Practice right, I say, like this. Watch my lips!" And she took a deep breath and blew out on it. But the only result was that her face turned a marvelous red that I've never seen before, and the bugle let out a very strained "breeeeek" that sounded sort of rude. "Well now, I've lost the hang of it," she grumbled, handing it back, "but you do it something like that."

She harumphed again and looked the old attic over. "I reckon this place could keep you busy today, seeing as it's wet outside. Get dressed first." And with that she clumped downstairs.

"She's not so bad," Jack said, kicking his feet happily against the wooden sides of the old rocking horse and fingering his beloved bugle.

"Are you really going to learn to play that thing?" I asked.

"I already know how," he said.

"You sound like a dive bomber."

"It really is painful, isn't it?" he said, grinning.

After breakfast was over and the chores were done, we went back to the attic to see what was up there. The first thing Jack found was an old shoe-shine kit that he quickly set aside. I figured he would ask Aunt Irene for it so that we could take it home with us.

"Lookee, Jack—harmonicas!" I called. "Hidden under these old boxes."

"Let me see one!" He took it and blew on it. It sounded old and horribly out of tune, but he was optimistic and tucked it in his back pocket.

I found an old buck's head in a corner. The wooden backing had come off, and I managed to get the thing on my shoulders without being knocked over by it. It gave me an idea. I found an old blanket to wrap around me, and then I held the buck's head on my shoulders, with my own head bowed down and covered up by the blankets. "Moo! Moo!"

"Penny," he yelled. "If I were as thickheaded as you, I wouldn't brag about it! Bucks don't say *moo!*"

But I kept charging at him and yelling *moo*, until he found a bear's head that our great-great-grandfather must have shot and mounted, and he came back barking at me with it until I left him alone.

"What *do* bucks say?" I asked when we sat down, laughing and panting from having run so hard.

"They don't say moo, I know that."

"Well, bears don't bark."

"Hey, you know what a chicken says?" he asked.

"No, what?"

"He says, 'Hey, don't hit me. I give up. I give up.' "
And then he laughed at his own joke. "Get it? He's a
chicken! Say Penny, look at this!" He jumped forward
over the rubble of blankets and the bear head. "It's
books!" He meant to pull the old carton of books closer,
but it was so dried out that it fell apart in his hands.
A half dozen of the fattest spiders you ever saw scurried
in every direction. "Get 'em, quick!" he yelled, forgetting
the books. I grabbed one by the leg and swung it so
it couldn't double up and bite me. These were big guys,
and for a minute we forgot the books in this new
discovery.

Jack spied a steel strongbox full of papers, and he
quickly shook them out. We slipped three of the spiders
inside and shut the lid. "Beauties!" he exclaimed. "Wolf
spiders!" He set the strongbox by the shoe-shine box.
"We can use those."

"How?"

"When it comes time to be resourceful, we will have
some resources, okay? Never waste anything," he said.
"Besides, I can sell them, maybe—a quarter apiece. Let's
find some more."

We hunted around on the floor and found a few
more in the attic corners—six new ones in all, so that
made nine. "I'll cancel your debt," he told me, "if you
remind me to feed them every day."

I agreed, and he went scrounging to see if he could
get more. One time he sat back to rest, and he sat right
on the harmonica in his back pocket. "Yee-ouch! Here!"
He fished it out of his pocket. "Can you find a safe
place to put it?"

I threw it into a box of rotting feather pillows and comforters, then turned back to the old books. The covers were leather, some of them cracked in places. Gently I pulled one of the books on the top closer, then lifted it onto another crate where the light was stronger.

I opened it. The first page had only a few lines written in a thick and clumsy pen.

Nils Augustus Holmes
His five-year diary
Being sixteen years old this day
From
Mother and Father, with love

"Jack," I called. "It's a diary!" I flipped over a few pages to a short entry.

July 1st
Mother bought teeth. Says they are astonishingly good. Had the last of the venison stewed to celebrate. She says she enjoyed chewing. I wonder at the progress of science in this land, where new teeth can replace old so conveniently.

Jack wouldn't believe that the diary really said that, so I showed it to him. I read on for a while, mostly finding passages about the forests and the prospects of dairy farming, and then I came to another good entry:

August 8th
Our third day at the seashore. We waded in the surf some good time together. Mother walked in too far, and a wave struck her in the face so that she submerged. Father and Judson endeavored to find her, but she came up under me rather suddenly so that I fell in myself. Being

*more hardy, I recovered quickly, but she had lost
her teeth. Regardless of our clothing, Judson and
I proceeded to dive for them. I thought they were
lost forever in the churning surf and was wading
back to Mother, when Judson approached me with
the missing dentures displayed proudly on the
palm of his hand. Mother promptly tried to replace
them as she was most uncomfortable without
them. But Mother's gladness was short-lived as
the particular set of teeth that Judson claimed from
the ocean were not Mother's own. We tied up
the teeth that he had found in a scarf and went
to lunch. Mother ate soup.*

August 9th

*Visited coast guard with our teeth. A gentleman
thanked us for them and showed us his collection—
about thirty sets in all. He lectured Mother on
how foolish it is to wade with false teeth, for the
waters are treacherous and unpredictable. Indeed
he had found two sets yesterday. Yet he had little
hope that either could be hers, for he said they
had been discovered last night on the shore a
hundred and fifty miles away. His opinion proved
to be accurate. Mother will have to be fitted for
new teeth. Today she watched longingly as we all
ate saltwater taffy.*

I wanted to read more, but I heard Aunt Irene calling
us for lunch. I fished Jack's harmonica out of the feather
pillows for him; then we scurried downstairs to wash
and to eat.

"Aunt," Jack said at lunch. "Could I shine shoes
in town?"

Her steely eyes popped open in surprise. So did mine, I think. "Work?" she asked.

"Jack always has a job," I said. I stuck up for him to her, but I was a little annoyed.

"If it's all right with your father, yes," she replied. "But what about your sister here?" She glanced at me. Obviously, there was room in this town for only one shoe shiner, and any other jobs would be scarce.

"She can advertise for me," he suggested. "How about it Penny?"

I shrugged and nodded. "Sure." It sounded a lot better than sitting around the house. But I didn't want to spend the summer working in the town. I wanted to go explore the mountains. I glanced reproachfully at Jack, but he winked. He was onto one of his ideas.

"So you've found treasures in the attic," Aunt Irene rumbled. "I heard you knocking around quite a bit."

"What do bucks say?" I asked.

"Bucks! They don't talk. What a silly question!" And she squinted hard at me to see if I was making fun of her somehow.

"I mean what noise do they make," I said.

"Well, I've never heard one. I suppose they don't make any noises. You didn't find a buck up there, did you?"

"Just his head," Jack said. "The rest of him was missing. We found an old diary and some papers and junk, too."

"Ah, I think I should gather those papers and sort them today," she said, more to herself than to us. "It's high time I did."

"I found a harmonica, too!" Jack exclaimed, and pulled it out of his pocket. "Listen!" He blew a note, and a cloud of goose feathers shot out across the table and fell into Aunt Irene's soup.

"My stars!" Aunt Irene exclaimed. She glared at Jack as though he had done it on purpose. Jack looked back at her, scared. But it was my fault for putting the harmonica in those pillows. I was about to take the blame, but I couldn't get a chance to speak.

"Well, go along and get another bowl!" she told Jack. "I can't eat it with feathers in it. Go on!" Then she harumphed, but I saw the hint of laughter in her steel blue eyes. As Jack rushed into the kitchen, she muttered, "That boy's got a gift for music and a gift for disaster, and they've both shook up together inside him." Then she harumphed again.

Just then we heard a joyful, challenging bark. "There he is again!" she cried, leaping up. "Where's my cane?"

"But Aunt!" Jack yelled, coming in. "Aunt Irene! It's raining." Too late, she snatched up her cane and raced out of the dining room. We rushed to the window. The collie was back, barking at Aunt Irene. "Out of my roses, you villain! Scat!" And she swung the cane at him. He nimbly leaped aside and barked at her, his pointed ears laid back and his dark eyes laughing at her. He barked again. "Scat, I say, or I'll thrash you into next week!" She swung again, and he leaped back. She swung three or four times in a row, and each time he dodged, sidestepped, or leaped over the cane.

"That's the dumbest dog I've ever seen," Jack muttered. "Doesn't he know she's serious? If she lands that cane on him, she'll knock him cold."

She swung at him so hard that she spun around, and the dog got a mouthful of her hem. "Where are you? Where are you? Let go, I say! Let go!" But he was tugging around her in a tight circle so that she couldn't get her balance enough to whack at him. The wet grass was slippery, and he almost dragged her around in a circle. At last he let go and raced over the lawn toward the creek, his soggy tail waving in the gray mist. He stopped once, barked happily at her, and then galloped away. We raced back to the table and sat down. She stumped in, wiped her feet on the rag rug by the door, and resumed her seat at the table.

"I brought you your soup," Jack said gravely.

While we cleaned up from lunch, she went upstairs to get the boxes of papers she wanted to sort through. "I'll be at my desk," she called down to us.

We finished putting the dishes away and returned to the attic. Jack was still rummaging through boxes, but I had found my own gold mine. If I had to go hang around that one-gas-pump town, I would be sure to bring some of those old diaries with me. Apparently Aunt Irene's ancestors had all been very diary-minded, for that whole box contained nothing but old journals.

"Look!" I said to Jack. I held up one of the books and then read the flyleaf to him,

Presented this day to Bill Birky

On his sixteenth birthday, May 21, 1936

From his loving sister, Irene

"That's Uncle Bill," I exclaimed. "The one who's a lawyer out in California. Aunt Irene gave this to him when they were kids!"

Jack shrugged. "I like Nils Augustus better," he said. "He's a writer I could really get my teeth into." And he grinned.

"Uncle Bill tried bootlegging for a while," I told him. "I wonder if he wrote about it."

"Hey!" Jack suddenly turned. "Where's that strongbox, Penny? We've got an investment in there— two dollars and twenty-five cents worth of spiders."

"It's on the other side of the shoe-shine box," I said.

"No it isn't. It's gone. Help me find it. I don't want those things to starve to death."

"I thought I put it over there when we were going to lunch," I said.

He rummaged through the box of pillows. "Where could it be? You didn't throw it in here with my harmonica, did you?"

"No. I don't know where it is."

"Where could a strongbox be hiding?" he asked.

Just then an ear-splitting scream tore through the air. "My stars!"

I looked at Jack. "Aunt Irene knows," I said.

We rushed down the attic steps and up the hallway to her room. The door was open. "My stars! My stars!" she was shouting, and between her outcries we could hear a tremendous whacking.

"My spiders," Jack moaned. We burst into the room.

Aunt Irene looked white, and her eyes—for once— were perfectly round. "Get them! Get them!" she screamed. We rushed in. I dived and caught one before it scuttled under the bed. Jack flung two more into the strongbox. We slammed the lid down.

Nearly fainting, Aunt Irene settled back into her desk chair, fanning herself with one long hand. Jack touched her shoulder as though to say something.

"Waaagh!" she screamed, and leaped up.

While she was still trembling from the false alarm that Jack's touch had caused, another spider scuttled from its hiding place under the desk. "There's another one!" she cried, and flung a paperweight from the desk right on top of it.

"Ooh!" Jack moaned as another twenty-five cents bit the dust.

"How many have you killed, Aunt?" I asked, hoping to calm her down.

"That was the fourth—lands, no, the fifth," she gasped, but she wouldn't sit down again. Jack sighed.

"Well, that's almost all of them," I told her. "We've got three in the box right there. We only caught nine."

"You?" she stammered. "You?" I thought she might really blow her top then, but she only said, "Give my heart a rest, child. Don't bring any spiders into this house! I live in mortal fear of them. Lands, if I thought there were a single spider anywhere in this house, my poor heart would never bear it!"

"Why, Aunt," Jack said. "The attic is full—"

"Jack!" I barked, interrupting. "She doesn't want to hear what *else* we found up there!" And I stared at him, really hard. Poor Aunt Irene! She would have died on the spot if he had told her the attic was full of them— which it was.

He got my message. "Oh, of—of course not." Then his eye fell on the paperweight on the floor. "That looks like a hockey puck," he said.

"It is." She was still gasping. "My Justin was on the hockey team in the winters. He scored the winning goal of the championship one year with that puck, and he gave it to me to remember him by." Jack stooped and lifted it, then sighed at the remains of the spider. "Pucked to death," he muttered. "What a way for a beauty like you to have to die." And he sighed heavily.

I didn't have the heart to leave poor Aunt Irene alone after that, so I offered to stay with her while she worked on the papers. Besides, according to my count, there was one more spider hiding somewhere. I read through parts of Bill's diary while she worked, but I couldn't concentrate, because every now and then a wisp of her hair might come loose from its knot and strike her neck, and whenever it did, she would think it was a spider and leap to her feet screaming, "My stars!" Or else she would just imagine there was a spider on her and she would yell "Waagh!" and slap herself. It was an unsettling afternoon, and I hoped my father would call soon.

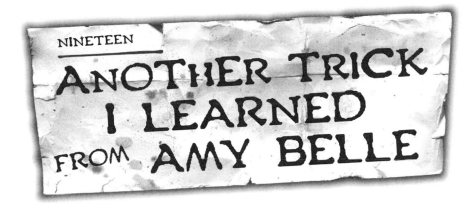

NINETEEN

ANOTHER TRICK
I LEARNED
FROM AMY BELLE

"We're working today," Jack announced at breakfast on Monday morning. He swabbed his toast around in his egg yolk. "You sure make good breakfasts, Aunt Irene." To my surprise I saw a smile flit across her face as he crammed half the toast into his mouth at one bite. But she only said, "So you're going through with your shoe shining, eh?"

"Yes," he told her. "And we'll be at it until suppertime if that's all right."

She ducked her head to agree. "That's fine."

Aunt Irene said she would do the dishes that morning, so Jack went to get the shoe-shine kit, and I went to get Uncle Bill's diary.

The phone rang while we were upstairs. I thought it might be Dad, so I ran to the top of the stairs. Aunt Irene was saying, "Eh? Yes, it's me. He is? And not much food, either, I'd guess. Well, there's no telling. No, I haven't seen Sam—wasn't in church yesterday. Could be they've gone off together—wait a minute. Penny, Jack, hurry along now! Time's a-wasting!" she called.

Jack came hurrying down the hallway. We went down the stairs and out the front door. I told Jack about what I'd heard. It didn't sound suspicious at all, except that Aunt Irene had wanted us out of the house before she continued the conversation.

"Maybe she knows something about that kid," I ventured.

"Only way we're going to find out is to find him ourselves," Jack said.

"You figure on getting good business?" I asked him.

"Sure. Didn't we meet half the town in church yesterday?" he asked. "They'll come in droves—everybody's wondering how we're managing at Aunt Irene's." And he laughed. He pulled Humphrey the snake out of his pocket and let him twine around the handle of the shoe-shine box. I eyed Humphrey distrustfully. Jack had assured me he wasn't poisonous, and I suppose Jack would know because he'd been bitten by Humphrey five or six times already.

"What's so funny?" I asked as Jack kept laughing.

"The storekeeper," he told me. "Mr. Lamerson. He was right."

Everybody in town called Mr. Lamerson Sam, but Aunt Irene said we had to call him Mr. Lamerson because he was an elder in the church and a very wise man.

"Right about what?" I asked.

"About Aunt Irene. He told us she was soft on the inside, and she is."

"I think your x-ray vision must be working better than mine."

He rolled his eyes at me. "Come on, Penny. She grumbles a lot, but it's not everybody who can withstand nine wolf spiders running around her room."

"Eight, Jack, eight. We haven't found the ninth one, yet, and we'd better hope that she doesn't find it either." But I knew he was right. She hadn't punished us—hadn't even said anything about it when Dad had called.

But I was in a bad mood and sighed. "Well, I hope Mr. Lamerson tells us some good stories today, because it's going to be boring loafing around town today while you shine shoes."

"Nonsense," he said. "Can't you see the perfect cover when it hits you over the head?"

"What hit my head?"

"A cover, a cover. This is our cover, Penny. We're the two innocent visitors, working our way through grade school by shining shoes, but nobody knows we're officially deputized detectives, right?"

"Right," I said sourly. "Deputized detectives."

"Yeah!" he exclaimed, annoyed. "And don't act so grown-up and grouchy! You're the one who likes Amy Belle so much! This is how we're going to find out who that red-haired kid is. First, we case the town, narrow the citizenry down to a few shady characters, and then keep the heat on them until one of them coughs up the red-haired kid." He pulled the bugle out from under his jacket. "We've always got our secret weapon to help us!" he exclaimed. He had tied it to a string that he wore looped over his right shoulder.

It sounded like a pretty sketchy plan to me, but I didn't say anything. We arrived at the town before the gas station and store were open. Jack wandered around, trying to find a place to set up his business.

"Why not in front of Lamerson's?" I asked. I remembered how nice it had been to be set up so near the quick mart. Memories of pretzels and hot chocolate were making the whole idea sound a little better.

"Because shady characters don't wander around in the hub of the town," he said. "We have to go to a place that's not so obvious—that alley over there." He pointed to a narrow alley across the street. We went over and set up the stool and box right in the mouth of the alley, and then we sat down on the plank sidewalk. "We're lucky," he told me. "We staked out the only alley in the whole town."

We sat and waited for customers, but the few people who were out on business just kept walking past. At last we saw Pastor Killian walking our way.

"Here comes the pastor!" I exclaimed. "He'll give us some business!"

"I hope he's got black shoes on," Jack mumbled. "That's the only color we've got until Lamerson's store opens."

Sure enough, Pastor Killian came up, and he had on black shoes. "Have at it, Jack," he said, putting his foot up on the box. "How are the Derwood kids today?"

Pastor Killian was young and bony, with a big Adam's apple that bobbed up and down when he talked. But Aunt Irene thought he was wonderful, and I knew that a lot of the ladies in the town baked and cooked for him.

"He's so sincere," they said at church and smiled at him. He worked night shifts in a zinc mine about ten miles away because the church was too small to support him.

"We're fine, Pastor," Jack said, smearing on the shoe polish. "What's the word around town? Anything going on?"

"Olaf Shulz's cat had a kitten born with six toes on each paw," he replied. "I reckon that might make the papers." Jack took out a rag, snapped it by pulling it tight really fast, and began shining the shoes. He'd been spending the weekend practicing his technique while I had posed for him with one of Uncle Mickey's old shoes on top of the box.

"You don't say," he drawled, but he glanced up, hoping the pastor was noticing how smartly he was shining the shoe.

"Let's see. Judson Groff was giving a cookout Saturday night. When he bent over the hot dogs, his brand-new toupee dropped off his head and into the coals. But everybody knew about that before it got to the papers." Pastor Killian smiled.

"Any visitors at church?" Jack asked.

"You two."

"Oh yeah. Ha-ha, us." He let Pastor take his foot down and put the other shoe up on the box.

"There's news," Pastor said suddenly, looking across the street. We turned around but didn't see anything.

"What?" I asked.

"Sam's store isn't open. I can't remember a day when he's been late before. Wasn't in church yesterday, either."

Jack looked at me. Sam Lamerson knew something about the red-haired kid. Were they together?

Pastor noticed the look. "You kids met Sam yet?" he asked.

"Last week," I said. "He told us stories about the old days."

Pastor nodded. "From what I understand, your Aunt cleaned up this town pretty well. She's quite a lady."

Another obvious comment about Aunt Irene. I nodded. "True."

Jack snapped the rag to indicate that he was finished. "What do I owe you, old man?" Pastor Killian asked.

"Clergy goes for free," Jack said, shyly. He knew Pastor was poor.

Pastor Killian smiled again, his big face-splitting smile that made his Adam's apple stick out even more. "I'll be a steady customer then." He nodded toward the store. "But if you two detectives are after news, Sam's the man for that. He can tell you anything you want to know to solve your case." And he walked away.

Jack sat back on his heels. "I thought I was so subtle!" he exclaimed. "He saw right through me!"

Jack played with Humphrey awhile, then put him inside the shoe-shine kit for a rest. We sat and waited another half hour for customers. Jack was dejected, wondering how Pastor Killian had seen right through our cover. I was about to turn to Uncle Bill's diary when the door to Lamerson's store was pushed open and a hand turned the sign from Closed to Open.

I nudged Jack. "Lamerson's finally opened up."

"Huh? Oh, yeah. Here." He handed me two dollars. "Could you get some brown shoe polish and some maroon?"

"Sure." I trotted over to the store. Nobody was at the register. I wandered back to the household goods shelf and found the flat, disk-like cans of shoe polish. Nobody had yet come to the counter, so I rang the little bell by the cash register and hoped Mr. Lamerson wouldn't think I was rude for doing it, but I wanted to get back to Jack.

I heard footsteps and dug into my pocket for the money.

"That all?" a gruff voice asked.

I looked up in surprise. I was face to face with one of the men who had tried to kidnap Jack at the train station!

He must have seen my surprise, because he said, "Sam's gone to Peoria to be with his mother. She's sick. I'm his nephew Lou."

So he didn't recognize me; I was sure of that. But I knew he was lying about Sam. I just shoved the money across the countertop. He was the skinny one, the one who had yelled that Jack wasn't the right kid. Where was the big bearlike one?

As though in answer to my question, the big man came down from behind the canned goods. He stopped in surprise and looked at me a moment, and I thought the game was up. He's recognized me, I told myself, and now they'll know that I know they're lying. But he was only surprised to see somebody there already. He didn't recognize me, either. I knew I had to get Jack and get out of town. The big guy would surely recognize him after having almost kidnaped him.

Once again, all the Amy Belle was oozing out of me in the face of danger. I decided we could find the sheriff or let Aunt Irene take care of the whole mess. But then my eye went to the big windows behind the counter, and I felt my heart drop into my stomach. There was Jack, trotting over to the store!

There was no way to warn him. I was too far from the door to run for it. "Wait a minute," I said to the mugs behind the counter, and I ducked behind the shelves of canned vegetables. If they jumped Jack again, I was going to get plenty of ammunition to fight back with.

I heard him walk in while the two men grumbled under their breaths about something to each other. I heard Jack's gasp, and I grabbed a can of vacuum-packed pineapple slices in each hand. The two men at the counter roared in surprise at sight of him. They had been casing the town, I thought, and figured he was gone. Oh, what had they done to Sam Lamerson?

WA-ANG-ANG! Jack's bugle cry split the air, momentarily shocking the men and making my head split. "Where's Penny?" he cried.

"Here, Jack, run for it!" I yelled. I flung the pineapples at the two men while Jack raced out the door.

"Get her!" the bearlike man yelled while he raced out the front door toward Jack. Jack raced out, blowing as he went—WA-ANG-ANG! The thin man was coming around the counter to get me. I ran up the aisle toward the back, pulling cans of fruit down to the floor as I went. I turned to throw some at him as he came around the corner, but I didn't have to. He slipped on a can and went down, and I found my way through the back door.

Their car, an outlandishly big Cadillac, was parked behind the store. The driver's door was unlocked. I jerked it open and thrust my only weapon—a can of cling peaches—under the brake. Then I ran blindly along the back of the store and behind the bank. Jack and I nearly crashed into each other. "Penny!" he cried.

"Come on!" I pulled him after me the other way, past the big Cadillac again, just as the skinny man emerged from the back of the store. Out of the corner

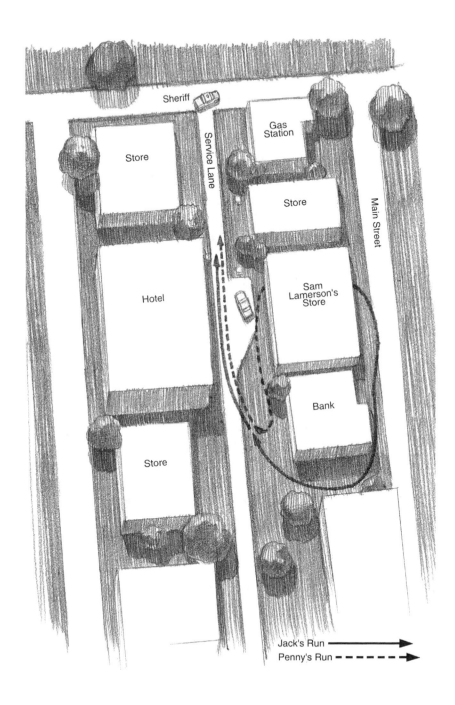

of my eye I saw the big man come around the corner of the store behind us. We ran straight down the service lane and kept our head start.

"We have to turn," Jack gasped. "They're getting into their car to chase us! Let go!" he cried. He meant to run where a car couldn't go.

"No, Jack!" But I was too breathless to explain. I kept my grip on his wrist as we ran. I looked back. The car was coming to life. It started after us, picking up speed. I could see that the driver meant to pass us and then cut us off.

"Now!" I yelled. I slammed sideways into Jack and knocked both of us out of the dirt road and behind some garbage cans. The car skimmed past, and I could see the surprised faces of the two men as they went by. The skinny one was at the wheel, jerking up and down as he tried to hit the brake.

Somebody must have heard Jack's bugle and called the sheriff, because at that moment the sheriff's sleek tan-and-white car slid up across the mouth of the service lane, and the sheriff stepped out.

"No, no, run!" I called in horror. Jack blew for all he was worth.

WA-ANG-ANG! He hit that frequency that gave me a headache. Apparently it could do more than just that. A window pane above us shattered. The sheriff leaped to the side. And the black Cadillac glided smoothly into the side of the sheriff's car and sat there, imbedded.

The two thugs jumped out, and the sheriff—wisely—tackled the thin one.

Jack and I charged after the bearlike one. Jack was blowing for all he was worth—WA-ANG-ANG! WA-ANG-ANG! He hit an especially high note—WA-ANG-

ANG! I saw stars; another window on the left side above us burst into splinters. After a minute I couldn't stand the bugling any more. I dropped out of the chase. Surviving windows were being thrown open, and heads were popping out all over town.

Suddenly Pastor Killian went dashing past me, muttering, "That boy's a fool!" In a trice his long legs had caught up with Jack, and he pulled Jack down. I ran up.

"What'd you do that for?" Jack asked.

"Do you think I was going to let him lead you out in the woods? You're no match for him!" Pastor cried.

"Help was coming!" Jack insisted.

"Not soon enough!" he exclaimed. He shook Jack's bugle at him. "You'd better learn to think, son. That man's desperate, and you were headed right out of town!" He looked like he wanted to say more, but he didn't. Somehow I got the idea that Pastor Killian knew something about those men.

Jack was ashamed.

"Come on," I said gently. "Thanks, Pastor." We walked back to the sheriff.

"Six thousand dollars of government property," the sheriff was roaring at his culprit. "Now what were you doing joy riding down a service road?"

"He tried to kidnap me!" Jack exclaimed, pointing at the man.

"A lie!" the man exclaimed. "I caught the two of them fooling with my car. When they ran away, I chased them and couldn't use my brake!"

"That's not true!" I exclaimed. "I didn't do anything to your car until that big guy chased my brother! And you were chasing me!"

"She's right, sheriff!" a woman in the gathering huddle of people said eagerly. "I was just coming in and saw the big one chasing the boy out into the street."

"He was shoplifting!" the man returned.

"I was not! Check my pockets!" Jack retorted and lifted his hands to be searched. "And no shoplifter would blow a horn for help!"

"Put your hands down, son," the sheriff said. "If Lamerson says you were shoplifting, I'll search you."

"Sam Lamerson's gone," I said. "And this man says he's Sam's nephew, but he's not!"

The sheriff eyed me. "Oh he's not, eh?"

"No," Jack said. "This one and the big guy tried to kidnap me the very first night I was here, as soon as I stepped off the train. My Aunt Irene chased them away."

Nearly everyone in the crowd suddenly said "oooohh!" Jack and I glanced at each other.

"That'll be *your* aunt then," the sheriff said, and he touched his cap.

"Y-yes," Jack stammered.

"The nasty lady with the cane!" a little boy exclaimed.

"She is not nasty!" I snapped.

Jack nudged me. "Easy, Penny."

"No, she's not that," the sheriff said. "Your Aunt Irene's quite a gal. Come along. Let's go to the office and call her. If you're kin to her, I know you're all right." He handcuffed the man and started to get into the wrecked car. "Oh," he said, stopping himself. He looked around, embarrassed, then cleared his throat. "Let's walk."

He left a deputy with the two wrecked cars, and we all marched down to the sheriff's office. But first Jack and I picked up our gear from the shoe-shine box. Jack lifted the lid. Humphrey was fine.

TWENTY

WORKING TOGETHER WITH AUNT IRENE

Jack was the first one to speak in the car. "Are you angry with us, Aunt?"

She looked surprised; then she scowled. "Is your story true? Just like you told it?"

I nodded.

"Well, no then," she said. "You did what was smart and handy."

"I didn't mean to break all those windows," Jack apologized.

"It's a talent," she muttered. He looked down, and she added, "Windows aren't so much in a good cause."

"Those men aren't truant officers," I said after we were silent for a while.

She guided the car into the driveway. "No, and that little weaselly fellow is not a nephew of Sam Lamerson." Her jaw tightened. "I hope Sheriff Rimmel gets the truth out of him fast. Sam's in trouble, and those two are behind it."

"Sam knew something about that boy," I said.

Her scowl returned. "You kids have been reading too many books." She frowned at us. I should have taken her hint and dropped the subject, but I didn't.

"He told us not to get involved with that kid. He just about said he knew something about where that boy has come from and where he's going," I told her.

She only scowled some more. "Why, the boy was obviously a runaway."

"But you should have seen how Pastor Killian—"

"That's enough, Penny," she said sharply. "You two aren't the sure-shot detectives you think you are, so hold your horses in!"

Surprised, Jack glanced at her. I felt my face burn. We silently got out of the car.

My feelings were hurt again, and I went to my room to be alone. I just couldn't understand her. When it seemed like she was the most easy-going person in the world, all of a sudden she'd get grumpy and touchy. I still had the diary, almost untouched. I would read it, I decided, and stay out of Aunt Irene's way. No doubt she would be wanting to make up in a little while like she had before, feeling guilty about being harsh.

So I shut the door to my room and started reading. The first entry sobered me.

January 8th

No coal, no wood except a few logs for tonight and tomorrow. Justin brought home a couple rabbits, and we had them stewed. Irene insists that the Lord will provide. Bryce and Simmons caught me coming out of Lamerson's today empty-handed because they won't give me no more on credit. Bryce and Simmons offered to lend me ten, but I said no. Irene wouldn't touch liquor money, and they know it. They called me a mama's boy and a Sunday-school kid. Irene seems to read my mind.

Heard her tonight in her room, praying hard and crying for me. I'd rather starve than break her heart, but I don't know how we'll get by.

January 12th

Pulled down dead branches in the forest and brought them home. Last night's wind was a blessing, as Irene says. Refused to read the Bible tonight after dinner. Made Irene cry, but I figure, let God prove Himself now when we need Him. Mickey read instead. But Irene was in tears, and so was Gertrude and little Molly also, though they didn't know what was wrong. I dared Irene to throw me out and make me find my own way in the world. She wouldn't—said she would be throwing me right to the bootleggers, and she'd rather die than put me in their hands. Justin said he'd knock me down if I opened my mouth one more time to Irene that way. Felt like a bully. Felt miserable.

Awed, I read on and on about that terrible winter, seen through Bill's eyes only. To me he wasn't my uncle anymore. He was a kid like me.

It was long though, interrupted by a long tale of hunting through the woods and descriptions of how he got little odd jobs here and there and how he performed them. I flipped ahead until my eye caught the names *Bryce* and *Simmons* all over the pages. Then I took up reading again.

June 2

Meeting Bryce at midnight. Left a note and all my money on the ironing board for Irene. It will be one less mouth for her to have to worry

*about, I figure, and I don't mind selling that stuff
to people who have the right to buy it if they
want to. Bryce tells me I will be a rich man in
a month. No more bread and syrup for supper.*

Then there was a long absence of days, and the
account took up in August. He had written about a
gun battle against other bootleggers, only he called them
criminals now.

August 6

*Jamison is dead—him with a broken-hearted
wife and two children in the next town! My mind
won't let me sleep. How many other people under
the stars tonight are broken-hearted because of
what I've been selling? How many wives without
working husbands? How many children with
fathers deep in drink? And Irene. I broke her heart
when I left home. What's happened to Justin and
Mickey—and little Molly!*

August 7

*I'm going back at dawn when the others are
asleep. If Irene has a sensible brain in her head,
she'll throw me back out for what I've done in
these wretched hills. But if I know her, she'll take
me back. How I hope she will! I have prayed to
God for forgiveness of my sins and the salvation
of my soul, and I have with me two pistols stuck
in my belt. Bryce suspects that I aim to cut and
run, and it will be a desperate race out of these
hills, but they won't suspect it at dawn, and they'll
be asleep, mostly. I will go on foot, with only
this book and my map. For someday I may come*

*back and dig up what I've left here—if times get bad
again, and Irene needs it.*

Hurriedly I flipped forward in the book, looking for
another mention of what he had left. Had he buried his
money up there? The rest of the diary contained a story
of how he had come home after fighting his way
through the hills, but I wasn't interested in that. Then
there were stories of jobs he had found, quotations from
the Bible, and more stories of little things he had done
with his brothers and sisters. It was a five-year diary,
and I wondered if I would ever find any other mention
of what was buried in the hills. At last I came to
September 7 of the next year.

September 7

Bryce is gone, and I heard that most of the others have been caught and sent to jail. Let it lie there in the hills! I've marked their places with white birches, and my own with the palmetto. The big place I labeled with a huge hemlock, seeing as it's a symbol of poison also. How fitting.

There it was, all explained! I leaped up to look at the map on the wall. Yes—five white birches, three palmettos, and a single hemlock. "Jack!" I called, running into the hallway. "Jack!"

I raced down the stairs. Where was he? "Jack!" I yelled. I ran for the attic just as he came clumping down.

"What is it?" he asked.

"Buried treasure!" I exclaimed. "The map on the wall! This diary! It's all explained!" I showed him the map and the entry in the diary. "We should have realized that these trees drawn on here are symbols!" I exclaimed. "Palmettos don't grow around here for hundreds of miles! What dunces we were!"

"This is great!" he said. "Let's ask Aunt Irene if we can go hiking!"

We ran downstairs, through the living room to the front of the house. "She must be gardening," Jack said. We went outside. "Uh-oh," he said. I looked over his shoulder. Uh-oh was right. The collie was walking up from the creek, and there was Aunt Irene in the roses, her cane by her side. Jack winced, but we were silent until the dog came up behind her and touched the back of her neck with his nose.

"Waagh!" she exclaimed. She picked up the cane and swung it back at him. But today the dog didn't move. He gave before the blow, and it seemed like a light tap compared to what I saw Aunt Irene deal out to the kidnapers that night at the station. The collie sank to the ground. Jack and I gasped and ran forward. She had done it at last—hurt that beautiful, triumphant collie.

But Aunt Irene screamed too and tried to lift him. "Tige," she called. "Tige, what is it?" Jack and I dropped beside her and the dog. She pulled her hand up, wet with blood. "He's been shot!" she exclaimed. "Oh, and I hit him! Jack, there's an old bicycle in the shed. Get on it, boy, and fly for the vet. He's on his rounds this time of day. Leave a note on his door and ask around. Please, Jack!"

He didn't need any second urging. He fled toward the shed. "Penny, can you help me lift him?"

"Yes." I got under his big shoulders, and she circled his hips with her arms. We lifted him together, and I heard her talking to him, apologizing for having struck him. "Oh, Tige, I didn't know you were coming for help this time!" We got him inside, and she quickly arranged a blanket for him in a corner of the kitchen. She got water in a shallow bowl and poured some over his tongue. He opened his eyes, lapped a little more from her hand, and gave a tired wag to his tail.

"Who would have shot a beauty like him? Why?" she asked, stroking his head. "Tige, don't be angry at your old friend."

In about twenty minutes Jack and the vet came in. The vet pulled the long fur back and looked at the wound in the dog's shoulder. "Get the kids out," he said briefly. "I'll take it out here."

"Is it bad?" Aunt Irene asked.

"Hardly a nick of itself, but it's a couple days old by the looks of it." He was hurriedly filling a syringe. Jack and I left quietly.

We sat in the dining room, frozen to our chairs it seemed, while the minutes ticked by. At last the vet came out again with Aunt Irene, giving her instructions on caring for the dog. "And you'd better keep that dog close," he said at last. "Whoever shot him used a .38 caliber handgun. It wasn't a hunter taking a pot shot— maybe somebody with a grudge against the dog. Somebody with a chicken coop, maybe." She nodded. It was true that chicken farmers weren't often friends with dogs. He promised to come back in the evening and left with a nod to us.

"May we see the dog, Aunt?" Jack asked.

"He's sleeping now," she replied. She sank into a dining room chair.

"Is there coffee on?" I asked. "Can I get you a cup?"

"Thank you, Penny. Bring yourself a cup, too, if you want."

I tried not to look at the dog where he lay stretched out and sleeping. It didn't seem fair to stop and check him when Aunt Irene had told Jack no. I got the coffee quickly and came back out with it. Aunt Irene spooned sugar and dry creamer into it from two sugar bowls on the table. We sat back and drank. I had never had coffee before, and it tasted terrible, but I was determined to get it down, seeing how grown-ups drink it all the time.

"Imagine," she said at last. "Two days with a bullet in his shoulder. He came down the mountain to me, looking for me to help him." Again her steel-like eyes turned watery.

"Tige knows you didn't mean to hit him, Aunt," Jack said quietly.

"Lands, it's hard to think of the poor thing struggling so hard to get that little way. Two days to go barely five miles!"

Jack and I looked at each other. "How do you know it was only five miles?" I asked.

"He's all full of burs underneath from nesting on the topside of Granny's Mountain—the burs don't grow anywhere else for twenty miles."

"Why's that?" Jack asked.

"Birky's gang brought 'em in up there. They had their hide-outs up there, and it was their way to check strangers for cockleburs to see if they were up to any snooping around. In those days I pitied the stranger found with any cockleburs clinging to his pant legs. The deputies or the crooks would get him for sure." She stopped to drink some coffee. "It stands to reason that the dog was up there when he got shot. He certainly didn't climb up the mountain with a bullet in his shoulder just to rest. And if he'd been any closer on any even ground when he got shot, it wouldn't have taken him so long to get here."

I swallowed my coffee with such a hard gulp that I choked. I sucked in my breath, got a lungful of coffee, and gagged. I tried to cough and for a minute I couldn't.

"Lands!" she exclaimed, and gave me such a sharp cuff on the back that I saw stars. She shook me. "Penny, girl, can't you breathe?" It was hard to tell whether I could breathe or not, she was shaking me so hard, but I kept coughing. "Lands, Jack, she's gone and snorted a draft of coffee up her nose! Turn her upside down!"

"NO!" I yelled, and jumped out of the chair. One last cough and I could breathe again. "Please, Aunt, don't help me anymore. I'm all right."

For an instant she looked hurt; then she said, "I thought you were choking. What with poor Tige shot and you coughing—"

"I'm all right, I promise."

"I must get ahold of myself," she said. "I've got to go tell Tige's owners."

"Who are they?" Jack asked.

"Oh, a pack of rich fools up the turnoff a little way. They said they were keeping Tige to start a kennel, only they never did, and they let him run all over. I reckon they feed him well enough, but they let him roam."

"Is that how you met him?" Jack asked.

"Oh my, yes. I was so afraid of him the first time he came bounding towards me. I just swung and swung at him with my rake, and he thought I was playing, and just kept barking and grabbing my skirt in his teeth. How I screamed! But I couldn't hit him, it seemed. He was just too fast, and I didn't want to hurt him, only drive him off. He came every day, and for the first week I was terrified of him; then I got to see what a nonsensical clown he was and how he loved for me to chase him. I've been doing that two years now with him, almost every day." Her lip trembled. "Only today I really hit him, poor dog."

"He came right to you, Aunt," Jack said. "He must have realized after you hit him that you thought he was still playing."

"And he took water right out of your hand and wagged his tail for you," I told her. "He knows you love him."

"Well." She fished a tissue out of her pocket and wiped her eyes, no longer even able to harumph her way back to normal. "I must call them or see them."

"Shall I go with you?" Jack asked right away.

"No. You're a good boy, Jack. But I guess I've stood up to every sort of person before this. I can face Tige's owners. Check him every half hour until I come back, won't you? But I shouldn't be more than a half hour. And don't touch him. Don't disturb him."

We promised we wouldn't. My heart was thudding hard as she found her car keys and left. I felt sorry for her—but oh, I knew I had figured out something big! Had Jack figured it out, too, I wondered.

TWENTY-ONE

MEETING MOSES

"Don't you see?" I asked Jack as soon as she left.

"I see two elm trees and a rose bush," he said. "Because I'm looking out the window. What do you see?"

"The cockleburs! We already know that they grow in only one spot!"

"Right. The spot where the bootleggers used to hide out." Jack was getting interested.

"And we know that the dog was up there, right? He traveled two days from that spot."

"Yeah?"

"Well, we've seen Tige stuck full of cockleburs before—remember on the way back from town the day Sam Lamerson told us stories. The road to town runs through the valley on this side of Granny's Mountain. Tige had time to leave Sam Lamerson and run up the mountain before coming back that day. What's that tell you?"

"That Tige is used to going up to Granny's Mountain."

"And who would shoot Tige, do you think, while he was up on Granny's Mountain?" I asked.

Jack frowned. "As soon as we saw that Tige was shot, I figured that the big thug had done it for some reason. For one thing, Tige was shot by a pistol bullet. I can't think of anybody else around here who would bother carrying a handgun. These people are more used to rifles—for hunting."

We were silent, putting it together: the big thug shot Tige up on Granny's Mountain. Why? At last Jack said, "Unless that big guy is downright mean and shot the dog for fun, I would guess he did it because Tige attacked him for some reason."

"Let's get Bill's map," I suggested. "I want to see where that hemlock symbol is."

We got the map and figured out where Aunt Irene's house was. It was a good thing Bill had been a good hand at mapping. He must have been familiar with drawing maps from sketching out exact routes and hiding places for the bootleggers.

"Of course," Jack said. "Here's the figure of a granny in a rocking chair that he drew in as a cartoon, and here's the hemlock tree that stands for—let's see, what does his journal say?"

I picked up the journal and read out loud. "'The big place I labeled with a hemlock, seeing as it's a symbol of poison also.'"

Jack whistled. "What's that mean?" he asked.

"Hemlock is a symbol of poison," I told him. "He put the hemlock as a poison symbol over a place that he considered poisonous or dangerous."

"Or a place filled with poison—a place filled with moonshine. Their hide-out," Jack said.

"That's what he means by 'the big place.' There must have been one place where they stored most of their stuff before they shipped it."

"Maybe that big thug is hiding out up there—could be he found it."

"That, or somebody else found it and got caught by the thug. If Sam Lamerson and Tige and the boy were up there, and the thugs got the jump on them— maybe Tige attacked the thugs. So they shot him—two days ago. That would have been Saturday afternoon, maybe Saturday evening after Sam's store closed," I said.

"I get it," Jack added. "Sam Lamerson missed church yesterday. He must have gone up there on Saturday night."

"I wonder if he's okay," I said.

We were silent. Jack went into the kitchen to check on Tige.

"He's sleeping," he said.

"I hear Aunt Irene."

She came in a moment later, looking relieved. "When I told them about the shooting, they said I could keep him for a while. I hope they let me buy him from them," she told us. "How is he?"

"Asleep," Jack told her.

"Good, good. Well now, you two run out and play if you like."

"May we hike, Aunt?" Jack asked.

By this time I had my own suspicions of Aunt Irene. It seemed to me like she was hiding something, too. I wondered if she also was figuring out the case. I half-expected her to tell us no, we couldn't hike, but she surprised me. "Hike? Well, I suppose. Be back by dark if you aim to get any supper. Don't go too far."

"We won't." We scuttled out. Jack and I had no idea what three miles in the woods can mean. We had the map with us and set out eagerly. We stayed hushed and quiet, as though perhaps the woods were loaded with thugs. At first the trail was perfectly clear. It was a double-rutted fire trail, cut into the undergrowth, and kept fairly clean. It climbed steeply in places, and I suppose if it had been a hiker's trail we would have been climbing on hands and knees in some places, but it was graded for jeeps and trucks.

Still, the climb was long. Flies and mosquitos buzzed around us. Soon we were out of breath, but we hurried as much as we could. The trail stayed good for two miles, while overhead the sun passed by and began to dip into the west. Sometime during the hike I realized we would never get back by dark, but I figured that even if we turned around right there we would still be late. If we went over Granny's Mountain, we could get to town and call more quickly than try to return.

Then the wide trail curved off to our right, away from the hemlock symbol on the map. We checked the map and found a deer trail that wound its way up in the direction we wanted. The summit seemed close, so we tackled it. We pushed past prickly branches that whipped back and forth, past thickets where unseen things rattled and buzzed.

Then Jack stopped. Ahead of us the trail faded out completely. "It's gone," he said.

"What is?"

"The trail." He consulted the map again, but I forged ahead into the stickly undergrowth.

"Wait, there must be a mark, something to make it apparent," he muttered. I came back and looked down. There were some burs stuck into my socks.

"We're on the right track," I said. I felt terrible and wanted a drink, but I didn't say so. Ahead of us the trees and thickets grew so closely together we didn't see how we could force our way any farther, and it seemed too wild to have anything like a big hide-out nearby.

"It looks impossible," I groaned.

Jack nodded. "Maybe that's how it's supposed to look," he said. He dropped to all fours. Then he got on his stomach. "I found it!" he exclaimed. "It's all overgrown, but we could push our way through."

I dropped down beside him, and he made room for me to look. Sure enough, a crawlspace had been cut into a thicket.

"Let's try it," Jack said.

"I hope there's no snakes in there," I whispered.

Triumphantly, Jack pulled Humphrey out of his windbreaker pocket. The snake coiled around Jack's wrist and stuck out his tongue, vibrating it.

"You can't keep him in your pocket. You'll squeeze him, and he'll bite you again." I was still whispering. Jack didn't seem to be afraid, but I didn't know what we'd find in that thicket.

"I know." Jack hurriedly took off the windbreaker and tied the sleeves around his waist. Then he wrapped it up like a little pouch and dropped Humphrey into it so that the snake rode comfortably in the small of Jack's back. "Just keep your head down, fella," Jack told him. Jack dived in first, and I followed.

We stomached our way for a long time. My arms got so tired I could barely drag myself forward. But we crawled along, and all around us insects buzzed and small things scurried away.

At last Jack stopped.

"What is it?" I whispered.

"A sod hut," he whispered back. "I'm looking for the thug."

We waited. At last I said, "Jack, he wouldn't sit inside a bug-infested sod hut if he was here."

"That's true. Let's risk it." He was as impatient as I was to know if we'd found the right place. He pulled himself out of the bushes, then helped me out. I saw one low, manmade construction built up of earth and sod. Stones lined the bottom of it. There was a door but no windows.

"It may have been made this way to turn aside bullets," Jack whispered. We walked stealthily along it and found holes worked into it here and there so that men on the inside, armed with rifles, could have lain on the floor and kept up a gun battle under the cover of the heavy stones. Jack understood things like battle strategy better than I did, and he explained it to me.

There didn't seem to be anybody around, and so at last we worked up our nerve to look inside. We came up on either side of the construction, edging to the sides of the doorway at the same time.

When we edged up to it, we could see that at one time there had been a heavy wooden door across the front of it. We saw the hinges, for one thing, but the door had either rotted away, or it had been used long ago as firewood. We peeked inside.

By now the sun was decidedly sinking, and we could barely see. We stood for several moments in perfect silence, straining our eyes. Suddenly I was scared. We'd done a foolish thing to come way up here, especially when it was getting dark.

"If you two stand there for one minute more, I'll bite my ropes off!" a voice said. We both jumped and almost screamed, but we caught ourselves. It was Sam Lamerson's voice. "What are you doing here, you reckless colts?"

Jack relaxed at the sound of rebuke. "We came up looking for you. Tige found his way to our aunt's house, and we figured out the rest."

"Irene? She sent you up?"

"Oh, no, we came up ourselves." And we plunged inside. The floor was rough and splintery wood. A little bit of light spilled in through a smoke hole and through the rifle holes. Our eyes adjusted to the darkness. Sam and the red-haired boy were tied up—leaning against the sod wall. Jack got out his knife and went to work on their ropes.

"We didn't take your advice," he said.

"You still may live to regret it, even though I'm glad to see you. This boy here is Moses. He's a little shy around new people, but he'll warm up to you."

I gasped.

"Moses!" Jack exclaimed. "*The* Moses?" We gaped at the boy.

"Don't be a lunkhead," Mr. Lamerson began. "*The* Moses lived thousands of years ago—"

"No, not that one. The Moses on the loading dock," I said, then explained. "We thought Moses was a code name for a member of a gang of smugglers!"

"Oh no. They captured him—well, now, I'll have to explain it all later," Mr. Lamerson replied. "Right now I'd like to know how you two figured out where we were."

"We had maps from the bootleggers," Jack told him. "And Tige gave us plenty of clues. Aunt Irene figured he had been shot somewhere up here, and we figured he must have been with you on Saturday night when he got shot. We came up to see for ourselves if you were still up here."

"Reckon I am, and I'm starving. That no-account gave us water, but not much food—some to Moses here, but none to me. Say, what happened to his partner?"

"My brother and I took care of him," I said carelessly.

Mr. Lamerson snorted. "Oh you did, huh? How?"

"Cling peaches," Jack said for me. "It never fails."

That puzzled Mr. Lamerson so much that he didn't know what to say. We got him and Moses free and rubbed the circulation back into their hands and feet.

"Now all we have to do is get back to town and be heroes," Jack said smugly. Just then we heard a crashing in the underbrush outside. "Like I said, now all we have to do is capture one armed thug, subdue him without any weapons of our own, get back to town, and we'll all be heroes."

"There's one thing that goon doesn't know," Mr. Lamerson whispered fast. "This place was used by bootleggers, and there's a cellar down below. Give me a minute to find the entrance."

He scurried quickly across the floor, feeling with his hands and tapping. Hurriedly he lifted up two stale and musty-smelling planks.

"May be snakes or something," he whispered. "I'll go first and test the ladder."

We nodded. Moses looked anxiously at Mr. Lamerson, but the storekeeper gave him a reassuring grip on his shoulder and hurriedly descended. "Come on quick," he whispered hoarsely. "It feels pretty sturdy." Then we heard a crash. "Ouch!"

We peered over anxiously. "Nothing at all," he whispered up. "Third rung from the bottom gave out. I'll help you down."

Jack and I made room for Moses to go down next. While I helped him get his legs going the right way to find the rungs, Jack crawled to the doorway. It was nearly pitch black inside the sod building, and a sort of purplish twilight outside.

"Hist," Jack looked back. "I see him worming his way in."

Moses' head disappeared down the hole, and I heard Sam Lamerson catch him. Then, because the thug was coming and I would have been caught going down anyway, I simply covered up the hole with the planks, brushed dirt across it with my fingers, and joined Jack.

Jack rolled on his side, even with the crook almost on top of us, and whispered in my ear. I thought he would say something like "Good-bye, dear sister, if one of us is killed." But instead he said, "Amy Belle, page 38." And then he ripped my jacket half off me. I caught his drift just in time. The thug had pulled some twigs from the thicket and was squatting right in front of the door to the hut, with his back to the dark entranceway. He must have been building up a small campfire.

We moved as quietly as possible and got my jacket off; then on flat palms and quivering knees we stationed ourselves on either side of the open doorway, each of us holding a sleeve of the jacket.

I figured the guy was confident that everything was okay and nobody could find him here, because he took his time. But at last he lit the kindling, then stood up and came inside to get his food—which must have been lying along the wall somewhere.

Just as he stepped inside, we jerked the jacket tight and pulled it up about six inches. He sprawled forward on his face.

We didn't know it, but Sam had climbed back up the ladder and was peeking out from a crack between the plank and the floor. As soon as the giant fell, Sam came up fighting like a wildcat. And while all three of us were fighting with this thug on the floor, Moses came up the ladder like lightning and bolted out the door of the hut.

"Let 'im go! Let 'im go!" Sam shouted. "It's the boy they want!"

I didn't know what he meant by that, but there wasn't time to ask. I had the guy by one of his massive arms while Jack and Sam wrestled with him. The whole mass of us pushed and fought until we were half-in and half-out the doorway where the light from the fire was spilling. Then suddenly the big guy gave a yell and threw both Jack and me off, and I thought he'd break Mr. Lamerson in two.

Early in the fight Jack's windbreaker had been ripped off, and poor dizzy Humphrey was sitting (or lying— it's all one to snakes) nearby, trying to collect his brains.

Jack grabbed him up as we dived into the struggle again. For a long moment or two nothing happened. Then all of a sudden the big thug screamed and grabbed his leg where Humphrey the snake had gotten a good hold. That was when Sam Lamerson deftly reached right into the guy's jacket and pulled out the .38 he carried in a shoulder holster.

"A-all right there, y-you mister cr-crook, you. J-just hold still!"

Jack pulled Humphrey off, and there was the thug, looking mad and scared. He pointed at the snake. "A viper?"

"Humphrey?" Jack asked. "Poisonous? Never! He's my buddy!"

But the snake was not feeling like a buddy, and he gave Jack a good bite on the hand. The thug looked really mad when he realized he'd been tricked by all of us. Then he got really scared when he saw that Mr. Lamerson didn't know the first thing about handguns.

Without warning the gun went off.

Mr. Lamerson almost dropped it. He shook so much at what he'd almost done that we thought it might go off again in his trembling fingers. "E-either one of you kids know anything about guns?"

"I know! I know!" the thug said. "K-keep your fingers steady. Hold the first finger alongside the trigger guard instead of pressing right on the trigger. That way you won't shoot me accidentally!"

"You tellin' the truth, buster?" Sam was serious.

"Yes! Yes! Ask the-the children here! They're Americans!"

Then I realized that the thug wasn't. He spoke with an accent.

"Where you from, anyway?" I asked.

"You are not entitled to know this!" he exclaimed.

The gun went off again in Sam's hand.

"Along the trigger guard you say?" Sam Lamerson asked. "I wish't I had my spectacles! Didn't bring 'em when I thought it would be a short walk!"

"Sorry," the man said quickly. "I come from a little village—only boy in the family to go to college! My mother's pride and joy. You know what it's like to have your own dear mother—"

Jack and I shook our heads. "Our mother died," we said. Of course we didn't say anything about our perfectly good second mother. We wanted to see this guy sweat a little.

"But you wouldn't shoot me because of that?" he asked.

"I wouldn't shoot you on purpose at all," Sam Lamerson said. "Not if you behave, but see I don't know much about guns and—oh—I just know it will go off again."

Finally Jack took the gun from him. Jack had taken a gun safety course with our dad once. "I think I've got it figured out, Mr. Lamerson," he said.

Then Jack told the thug to lie down and put his hands behind his back, while he held the gun ready. Sam Lamerson was still shaking, but he tied the thug's hands up real good. I don't think we had to worry about the thug trying anything. He was convinced our ignorance was just as deadly as his knowledge of guns. He didn't dare stir, and he winced every time Jack would shift his position.

"We'll likely pass a parcel of the night up here," Mr. Lamerson said.

"Penny, you might want to get some wood." Jack was his old self—taking charge. "Can you cook, Mr. Lamerson?"

"Now *that* I can do," Sam laughed, relaxing a little.

I built up the fire while Mr. Lamerson got "vittles" ready. "Can you explain what happened while you cook?" I asked.

"First off, I guess I better explain Moses himself," Sam began. He nodded in the direction the boy had gone.

"Yes, start with Moses." Jack gave me a knowing look that could have come from the cover of an Amy Belle book.

"He's the son of one of them, uh, physicians do you call them?"

"Physicist?" I asked.

"That's right. Well, his dad defected over here, you know, and our government gave him what they call political asylum. Somehow or another the boy got over, too, probably some secret way. Moses won't say to that. He's been trying to make his way to his father. But some lady agent he called Tom Thumb has been trying to steal him back so as they can force his dad to go back. He said she caught him once and you two got things all mixed up for this Lady Tom Thumb so he could escape. I reckon since he was having his own troubles with Tom Thumb he took special interest then and thought you were the most likely to help him, coming out like you did and bustin' up that smuggling ring."

Jack and I looked at each other, surprised.

"And we thought he was one of them!" Jack exclaimed. "We could have rescued him months ago!"

"Well, he followed you around a piece and somehow hooked a ride on the train coming East. Seems the agents that were after him almost got you by accident, you both being on the same train and all. So he ended up here, and I guess from what he said that he was watching you, getting ready to make contact when he thought it was safe. Only by that time he'd been into my store for food. I tracked him into the woods and heard his story, then gave him this place to hide. I've been trying to convince him that the closer he gets to his father, the more dangerous it will become. And I asked him not to contact you—didn't want you two getting yourselves into trouble. I think that the boy trusts me at last. He might stay put a while."

"But then this guy's an agent!" I exclaimed. "He'll let his country know where Moses is!"

Sam Lamerson laughed. "No he won't! No he won't. This guy and his partner have committed attempted assault and kidnaping of American citizens. Watch and see how fast their country disowns any knowledge of their attempt to kidnap the boy. I think we may have beaten them at last."

Sam was right—those mattress factory characters were still in jail. No foreign government had come to their aid.

He settled back happily.

* * * * * *

Along toward midnight we heard people breaking through the hedge of thickets and undergrowth. Moses appeared first, leading everybody. He flung himself at Mr. Lamerson and began chattering in some language mixed with English. Sheriff Rimmel was there, with Pastor Killian and a posse of other men. They swarmed all over the place. Most of them had heard of the bootleggers secondhand. They were as excited to find one of the old hide-outs as they were to capture an enemy agent.

"Where's Aunt Irene?" Jack asked.

"Waiting at home," Sheriff Rimmel said. "And like as not you'll get the licking of your life when you get home!" But he pulled our ears and slapped our backs and said we were a lot like her ourselves for pluck.

"What's pluck?" Jack whispered. "Isn't that for turkeys and geese?"

"It's guts," I whispered back.

TWENTY-TWO

RETIRED FROM AMY BELLE

Well, as it turned out, we didn't get spanked when we got home, and we were glad. Aunt Irene cried when she saw us and fixed us a dinner that would have done honor to the president. And while we ate, she couldn't take her eyes off either me, or Jack, or Tige, sitting in the corner dozing. I figured out that once you get Aunt Irene past her harumphing and clouting stage, she's a soft touch all the way through. When it came down to Jack and me almost getting killed, she was helpless.

Jack even asked her to give Humphrey a warm saucer of milk. She did it, too, but she made Jack take it to him.

We spent the next morning resting up and catching up on the news. As it turned out, nearly everybody we knew had been keeping the secret of Moses—even Aunt Irene, though she only knew that Sam had been helping feed the boy and hide him. She'd had no idea that Sam even knew where the old bootleggers' hide-out was. If she had, she wouldn't have let us hike around Granny's Mountain. It was also news to her that the map on Bill's wall had been a secret map to the old hide-outs and caches. She'd been around the map for years, and she certainly knew where at least a few of the secret places were in the hills, but she'd never bothered to figure out Bill's code or to even notice it much.

There would be hearings and testimonies given on the kidnaping, but Jack and I only had to write out testimonies that are called *affidavits* instead of testifying. They kept it all pretty quiet about Tom Thumb and who Moses really was—and Sam Lamerson got a neat letter from Moses' dad after the government got Moses and his dad together. The Federal agent delivered it right to Sam's store because nobody was allowed to know where Moses' dad was, at least not until our government agents caught up to Tom Thumb.

"Sam's gonna have *some* story to tell on those crates in front of his store," Jack said when Sam got the letter.

Now when Jack and I prayed together at night, we prayed for Moses and for Aunt Irene, too, because Moses had trusted us and because we weren't afraid of Aunt Irene anymore.

After a couple weeks we found out that Mom was doing better. She had to be in traction for a couple hours a day at home, but she thought we would want to come home after three weeks with Aunt Irene.

Aunt Irene told us about it in her harumphing sort of way, and said she could help us get off on the morning train, but Jack shook his head.

"What, and leave Tige behind?" he asked.

Her steely eyes looked hopeful. "You mean you want to stay the summer?" she asked. "I reckon he is a good dog, even limping like that, and I have gone and bought him. And of course, you'll be wanting to figure out that

foolish treasure map, though I've told you a thousand times already there's no money left up there."

"No point in wasting a good map and a good dog, though," Jack said, wagging his head. "Besides, our Mom can't cook yet, and you're a sight better at that than she is, anyway."

"Go along, you're teasing me!" And she cuffed him one.

I hugged her. "We want to stay because we want to stay," I told her. "Jack is teasing you."

She was so pleased that she could only harumph and wipe her watery eyes. Then she kissed us, slapped our backs, and told us not to meander underfoot, but play awhile with the dog so he wouldn't stiffen up.

But before I did anything else, I went upstairs and wrote a letter to Jean.

Dear Jean,

I'm sorry we won't be home right away. We plan to stay the summer. I know you've probably heard all you can stand about Jack nearly being kidnaped and our escapade with more foreign agents. I'm really writing to tell you that you can have all my Amy Belle books. I did learn one good thing from them—it's on page 38 of *The Moon Surface Oil Rig Caper*. Otherwise, I think I can live without them. See you in August.

Love, Penny

The way I figured it, with Jack as a partner and Tom Thumb on the loose, who needed Amy Belle?